**A GO**

Lisa Birnie
has worked as a journalist in Australia,
England, China, the USA and Canada.
Her book *Uncommon Will: The Death
and Life of Sue Rodriguez*, won Canada's
Hubert Evans Award for non-fiction and
is soon to be released as a feature film.

MW01141412

# LISA BIRNIE

# A good day to die

*To Sally and Michael,*
*Lisa B.*

*t*

TEXT PUBLISHING
MELBOURNE AUSTRALIA

The Text Publishing Company
171 La Trobe Street
Melbourne Victoria 3000
Australia

Copyright © Lisa Birnie 1998

All rights reserved. Without limiting the rights under copyright above, no part of this publication shall be reproduced, stored in or introduced into a retrieval system, or transmitted in any form or by any means (electronic, mechanical, photocopying, recording or otherwise), without the prior permission of both the copyright owner and the publisher of this book.

First published 1998

Printed and bound by Griffin Press
Designed by Chong WH and Anthony Vandenberg
Typeset in 12/15.5 Baskerville MT by J&M Typesetting

National Library of Australia
Cataloguing-in-Publication data:

Birnie, Lisa, 1928
A good day to die

ISBN 1 875847 75 8.
1. Death. Terminal care I. Title

306.9

This project has been assisted by the Commonwealth Government through the Australia Council, its arts funding and advisory body.

The poem reproduced on p. 186 is a translation by Kate McIlhagga from *Celebrating Women*, eds. Ward, Wild and Morley and reprinted with permission from the Society for Promoting Christian Knowledge, London.

# Contents

*To A. W. B.*

# Preface

The interviews conducted with patients, their families and the staff at McCulloch House were all given voluntarily, and with the knowledge that any information shared may be included in this book. Nothing of a personal or medical nature has been revealed without the express permission of the patients, family members or staff members concerned.

I am deeply grateful for their time, trust, humour and courage. Without their assistance, given, at times, under conditions of considerable stress, this book would not have been possible.

Lisa Birnie
May 1998

# Introduction

*Though they go mad they shall be sane,*
*Though they sink through the sea they shall rise again;*
*Though lovers be lost love shall not;*
*And death shall have no dominion.*
  —Dylan Thomas, 'And Death Shall Have No Dominion'

In the autumn of 1997 I was offered a writer-in-residency at
Australia's Monash Medical Centre in Clayton, Victoria.
The residency was specifically for McCulloch House, a short-
term palliative care centre that admits only patients who have
a terminal illness, need respite care, and/or are suffering unsta-
ble complicated pain or other symptoms. I saw it as offering an
education in the realities of death, and took it in a flash.

The contentious nature of all issues relating to death was
familiar to me. Three years earlier I had written *Uncommon Will:*
*The Death and Life of Sue Rodriguez*, a book on a Canadian
woman who had amyotropic lateral sclerosis (ALS), a motor-
neurone disease that leads to helplessness and death.

Sue, forty-one, a former athlete and mother of a nine-year-
old son, decided that when her voice started to fail she wanted
a physician-assisted suicide. Euthanasia is illegal in Canada, but

Sue fought for it all the way to the Supreme Court. Her argument was essentially about human rights. Suicide is not illegal in Canada, for obvious reasons, therefore those afflicted with restricted movement were discriminated against if legally denied the help they needed to kill themselves. Although Sue eventually lost, the publicity surrounding her fight, and the narrowness of the Supreme Court's five-to-four decision, created a public debate on euthanasia and physician-assisted suicide that continues unresolved in Canada to this day.

Sue asked me to write her story. Over several months I became intimately, if secondhandedly, aware of what it means to have no control over your body, to be locked in a wheelchair waiting for the release of death. Sue was receiving optimal palliative care at home, but she made it clear that it was acceptable only as long as she could control it. At the point where she felt there was insufficient quality in her daily life to make the struggle and monotony worthwhile, she intended to choose death. Quality of life, not quantity, was what counted. Sue's determination and courage on this point never wavered. Four days before her death Sue called and asked me to visit. She told me she had found a doctor willing to assist and would soon kill herself.

Sitting before her rigid body in its high-necked wheelchair, holding her bird-bone hands in mine, I reasoned that she was entitled to act out of her own lived experiences, to end her life according to her own reasoning. She, not I, was facing a slow decline into death, was unable to embrace her child, was locked in a wheelchair, confronting the monotony and humiliations of a life stripped of all control. Yet, as she methodically, confidently described her plans, I felt a fear, a wariness, a moral repugnance arise. I believed that nobody should have the authority to force a terminally ill patient who wants to die to continue to suffer. Yet I knew from my own lived experiences that if Sue eventually succeeded in having euthanasia legalised, it was inevitable that some patient who wanted to live would, without his or her knowledge or consent, be put to death.

Sue committed suicide using drugs, with the assistance of an unnamed doctor, on 14 February 1994. Commentaries, articles, and letters flooded the media. Opponents of euthanasia were often depicted as sadistic, right-wing, religious fanatics, while supporters were decried as godless pragmatists, enemies of the aged, and a threat to all handicapped. The hopelessness of formulating public policy that would not be legally challenged into infinity was apparent.

Sue showed an integrity and courage that never wavered. I was impressed by this but not bowled over by it. During the meeting of a parliamentary committee in Ottawa commissioned to study the recodifying of the Criminal Code, Sue appeared in a videotape arguing her case. Her question, 'Whose body is this?' became a rallying cry for those in support of euthanasia. It didn't do much for me. Every time I heard it a voice in my head quipped back with something like: 'Whose ever it is, it isn't yours. If it was, you'd be good-looking, rich, and immune to wrinkles and flu.' I couldn't see how you could claim ownership of something you hadn't created, hadn't bought, and over which your only ultimate control, albeit brief, was to exterminate it.

These were my emerging, troubling thoughts as I became progressively involved in the case. But I was sensitive to the fact I was writing Sue's story, and needed, for the sake of my own integrity, to honour the trust she had placed in me. In one sense this wasn't difficult. Sue was courageous, often funny, consistent in her beliefs and willing to accept responsibility for them. She believed totally in her own autonomy and had little respect for traditional authority, preferring to forge her own authentic morality. In this respect Sue was a quintessential baby boomer.

In another sense it was very difficult. I was troubled by the fact that Sue read little and had no interest in history, philosophy, literature or the arts. Most people don't, but most people don't try to rewrite law. Sue's total indifference to the impact her legal fight could have on society at large was striking. Several times she expressed the wish, vis-à-vis her legal action, that people should mind their own business the way she minded hers. Her view of life was essentially one-dimensional, whereas I couldn't accept the life of the body as an inclusive definition of human life. It was a natural outcome of Sue's way of thinking that legalised assisted suicide, euthanasia, was a logical, reasonable thing to do, in fact, a decent thing to do.

I didn't believe that logic and reason should be dominant principles in drafting laws regarding human life. Too many times in covering criminal and civil trials as a journalist I'd seen truth and justice slide between the cracks of logic and reason. The driving force behind their disappearance had been simple greed, which inhabits the human heart as naturally as bacteria inhabit our bowels. Greed has endless vitality and a thousand disguises. Our whole consumer society is based on greed. Simply watch family tensions rise when the owner of many possessions dies. No sooner is the body cold, than relatives start squabbling like a group of orangutans fighting over a banana. Even if the spoils have no real value.

I was also bothered by another element—the nomenclature of 'death with dignity'. Death with dignity involved killing yourself to avoid suffering. So far so good. But if you chose not to kill yourself and to endure physical suffering for whatever personal reason, why wasn't that also a death with dignity? Isn't our essential human dignity a facet of integrity?

Death-with-dignity proponents seem to believe dignity depends entirely on whether or not we can take care of our own physical needs. Who is it at such times who frets about dignity—the sufferer or the witness? This exclusive concept of human dignity seemed to me a ratty little thing, a prissy concept of what life and mankind is all about.

At the same time these ideas were stewing in my head I remained committed to the belief that anyone who preaches that avoidable suffering is good for the soul is a dangerous misanthrope. I see pain as a medically neglected, unmitigated evil, quite as capable of blowing away one's mind and soul as one's body. If we can walk on the moon, we can control pain. We just haven't arrived at that point yet, and the most potent reason why not is probably the historically pervasive belief in the whole of western culture that, because Christ suffered and died, suffering likewise raised one's moral status. This sadistic misinterpretation, which reached its apogee in the Inquisitions of the Middle Ages by burning people alive to purify their souls, has continued in society in smaller ways until recently. The flogging of prisoners, the beating of children to 'improve' them, are two examples. A more widespread and subtle example is the way in which we continue to tolerate pain. Here we are at the end of the second millennium and a prolonged, painful death is a nightmare common to us all.

And what of compassion, what of mercy? What would I do if my own child were terminally ill and in agony? I could not find an answer to these questions. Yes, I would beg the doctor to shorten the child's life and suffering. But what then of all my objections to euthanasia and assisted suicide?

After my book on Sue Rodriguez was released, my publisher set up a cross-country publicity tour of Canada. I was appalled at the evidence of terminal suffering that everywhere was presented to me. The extent of the ignorance of pharmacology and pain control among some members of the medical profession was disturbing. One woman's story was typical. Her mother died in agony of breast cancer. Three days before she died the doctor explained his refusal to give her sufficient morphine: she might, he said, become addicted.

When I returned from this trip, I dug into a medical library to try to understand the causes and reasons for this suffering. I concluded that doctors' fear of addicting patients, their lack of pharmacological knowledge, society's denial of death, the rigid taboo on any discussion of end-of-life questions, and the lack of any popular political will to do anything about it were the main causes.

In the face of these realities euthanasia has become widely perceived as a necessary good. The population is ageing, cancer rates are rising, and the first trickle of baby boomers will soon start sliding off the planet. The baby boomers, used to the good life and dedicated to the notion of autonomy, will consider euthanasia their right. Because I don't believe it is, I started looking for an alternative. Obviously, if euthanasia became widely and legally practised, the research to defeat pain completely would never be done. Was palliative care the solution? What was palliative care? How did it work? What were its principles? How good was it?

From this interminable interior debate I forged my basic question: *Is euthanasia either desirable or necessary, or might accessible palliative care supplant the need for it?* When the writer-in-residency at McCulloch House was offered, I saw it as a chance to answer this question. I would find an answer to satisfy myself, not from theory, but from those who were there in the middle of the crucible, doing the dying, the nursing, the doctoring, the feeling, struggling, and thinking about it.

I created a plan of approach. After spending a week at McCulloch House observing the routine and attending staff meetings, I drew up a standardised, basic, if rather open-ended questionnaire for interviewing the patients. It covered ten areas, with considerable built-in flexibility as to the type of detail pursued and the sequence of topics. Flexibility was essential because of the patients' varying energy and availability.

It soon became apparent that my planned approach might work elsewhere, but it wouldn't in a palliative-care unit. I had thought of dying as a passive state, something that happened *to* you, as if mind and heart had done all the exploring they were going to do. But I was wrong. Dying isn't just a question of our bodies falling apart but an experience of our whole humanity. As I interviewed the terminally ill, I found most aired their feelings easily, as if their hearts were wide open. Words they had spoken all their lives and roles they had played seemed to be undergoing a reassessment. There was a sense that they spoke out of their core, as if greater sharpness of internal vision now compensated for the declining strength of their bodies. Everything stored within a lifetime—love, hatred, serenity, bitterness, faith—stood to be aired, empowered, transformed, or even, as in the case of faith, lost or found at such a time. Dying, I realised, was a multifaceted, ongoing, *human* experience.

Nobody is left to die alone in palliative care. Dying is usually a family affair, a friendship affair, sometimes even a community affair, and always a staff affair. It is a time when the balance of relationships between patient, family and friends can be shaken. Old unresolved quarrels, loves, resentments and sibling jealousies can surge to the surface. The basic demands of people's daily lives are complicated and multiplied when someone close is dying. Transportation is required, families with small children move in, meals must be prepared as usual, leave must be obtained from work. This effort to keep going can create monumental stress.

I finally decided that the best approach was the simplest one: ask the patients, family, and staff to tell their own stories. Because of the personal nature of these stories, I have created fictitious names for patients and their families. Staff are identified by first name, with the exception of the doctors, whose real names are used. From these stories I would be able to categorise the various conditions the terminally ill patient faces such as unmanageable pain, a sense of powerlessness, grief, aloneness, hopelessness. I would be able to see what situations, conditions, and behaviours palliative care had in place to eliminate these obstacles to a 'good as possible' death. Patients' willingness to express their feelings as their life reached its end, and for families to speak from their position of loss, guaranteed a certain purity of fact and intent.

What I hadn't foreseen was the difficulty of working with the very worst cases of intractable pain. Most patients at McCulloch House were there because their pain had become uncontrollable despite normal palliative care. In the majority of cases the patient's pain was brought under control soon after arrival, but in other cases, particularly where there was a combination of physical, psychological, and spiritual suffering, the struggle to keep pain at bay was constant to the end and not always successful. I had to remind myself that these cases were as bad as it got. At the same time the views of McCulloch House patients or their families had added value because they originated in the actual experiencing, or witnessing, of a situation that had hit rock bottom. These were people living not on the fringes but in the very heart of suffering, the people to whom the question of euthanasia was most relevant.

That some of this material was 'proxy' data obtained from relatives retrospectively doesn't concern me. I wasn't attempting to write a definitive study of pain, palliative care, or bereavement based on 'factual' truth. Few people are capable of making clear, entirely valid statements during the terminal illness and loss of a loved one. When such a loss occurs, the nature of one's understanding of it can continue to evolve for years. Rather than concentrate on methodology or statistics, I decided to increase awareness of not only how people experience and deal with their own pain, but of how people experience and deal with pain in others. This isn't an area in which two by two necessarily equals four.

Interviewees were chosen at random. The willingness of the patient or family to discuss their experiences and their level of energy and availability were the only considerations. I interviewed staff members, wrote up a brief background profile of each, and noted their comments about working with the terminally ill, and their thoughts as to what palliative care can and cannot do. Always in the back of my mind was my basic question: *Is euthanasia either desirable or necessary, or could accessible palliative care supplant the need for it?* I had no idea how difficult this question would be to answer.

# Hope

*Work without hope draws nectar in a sieve,*
*And hope without an object cannot live.*
  —Samuel Taylor Coleridge, 'Work without Hope'

Twenty-one kilometres east of Melbourne, McCulloch House is on your right as you go through the main driveway of Monash Medical Centre. The two-storey red-brick building and its handsome wrought-iron balcony can be seen from Clayton Road, but a high wall hides a formal garden with lawn, some border plants along the paths and a few rosebushes. The trees and some of the bushes are older than most of Clayton's streets. This area is part of the original McCulloch House, built in 1874 as a convalescent home for women who needed 'good food and country air'. Today it is the administration and conference section of the palliative care centre. Dr Ruth Redpath and her husband, Bruce, were the chief co-founders of the reborn McCulloch House which opened to the public in 1996.

The new section, joined comfortably to a side wall of the old house, has a central core and two radiating wings. It was built in the generous well-lit style of a comfortable modern home. The furniture is traditional and comfortable—soft colours and linen chintz—and the flowers on the coffee tables are fresh. All the rooms in one wing have French doors opening onto the original garden, which results in a blending of the old and new buildings in a common stewardship of beauty. Patients in the second wing also only have to step outside their rooms to be in a garden, a more modern, lower-maintenance one than the original 'pleasure garden', but still abundant with the pleasure and peace that sun and soil can bring. Being able to walk in a garden, watch a breeze bend the flowers, or feel the bark of a tree are all part of being fully alive until death, which is the goal of palliative care.

What is palliative care? The World Health Organisation defines it this way: 'The total care of patients whose disease is not responsive to curative treatment. Control of pain or other symptoms, and of psychological, social, and spiritual problems, is paramount. The goal of palliative care is achievement of the best possible quality of life for patients and their families.'

The definition given by the Australian Association of Hospice and Palliative Care (AAHPC) is more encompassing: 'Hospice and palliative care is defined as a concept of care which provides co-ordinated medical, nursing, and allied services for people who are terminally ill, delivered wherever possible in the environment of the person's choice, and which provides physical, psychological, emotional, and spiritual support for patients and for patients' families and friends.'

Hope can play a critical role in determining the course of a terminal illness. It seems strange to speak of hope, but it is such a vital part of our human nature that, whether we are terminally ill or not, to be deprived of it is to have lost one's life already. In palliative care the concept of living fully until death is deeply tied into the idea of hope.

Hope is not, as I had been inclined to think, denial of reality. To be able to hope is to be able to wish, and wishing can carry power and meaning. Kate Fleming, a research and development nurse at the Churchill Hospital, Oxford, recognised this aspect of appropriateness in hope when she said that patients with terminal cancer hope they will not deteriorate further, that they will be able to 'keep going' with small daily tasks, that the doctor will continue controlling the pain, that their families will be well cared for and have good lives.

Despite all the expertise at McCulloch House, not all patients can be kept fully alive and comfortable right to the end. Ultimately all palliative care cases have a built-in, 'no win' aspect in that the physical outcome is predetermined, usually unwanted, and sometimes unpleasant. But even the worst scenario can be invested with beauty and power *if* carers have the freedom to act creatively, the wisdom to rely on one another, and the will to work for a common goal.

This freedom to act creatively as a team is a major characteristic of palliative care. In this it differs profoundly from highly institutionalised, acute hospital care. The character of palliative care has been shaped by a long history, starting with the hospice care system created and run by religious orders during the Middle Ages. It has always functioned outside the main structures of academic institutions and the medical establishment, and there is no good reason why this should change. Power and prestige are integral to established institutions, and a sort of hierarchical arthritis results. Andrew Hoy, editor of the *European Journal of Palliative Care* (*EJPC*), suggests that these institutions were established not only to uphold standards but also to protect their store of accumulated knowledge and the particular interests of the cognoscenti.

Palliative care has been less institutionalised and less intent on acquiring power and prestige than other specialties attached to vast institutions. And while it can tap and make use of their medical advancements, it remains populist in spirit and practice. Structures exist, sufficient for organisation and getting the job done, but teamwork dominates. This democratic teamwork approach leaves carers free to recognise and respond to the differing needs and situations in which the terminally ill find themselves. When a team is encouraged and allowed to draw on all its strengths, is willing to throw out all the rule books, gives the back of its hand to seemingly insoluble diffi-culties and gives free rein to the compassion in their hearts, the results in helping the terminally ill and their families can be awesome. The story of Sophia and Michael Fulton is one example.

'I was twenty-four and Michael was nineteen when we met. And, by the way, I'm Sophia, not Sophie. I'm not the Sophie type at all.'

Sophia Fulton's voice comes from the kitchen of her metic-ulously kept outer-suburban house. Cups and saucers rattle, and a moment later she is back in the family room with coffee strong enough to make one's heart sing. Tall and thin, brown-eyed and brown-haired, she moves with the suppleness of an athlete and the calm deliberation of a woman who knows her own value. She firmly tells five-year-old Andrew to keep the noise down, and settles thirteen-month-old Jonathan on the floor with some toys. Soon Jonathan staggers back onto her lap and pulls himself up. With a slight sigh and a kiss she keeps him there.

A faint smile flickers across Sophia's face. 'Where did we meet? In a nightclub.' She pauses. 'The way it turned out, he could have married someone else who'd have looked after him. But it was meant to be me. That I truly believe.'

Soon after, Michael moved in with Sophia and they lived together for four years before marrying. Her parents loved Michael, everyone loved him, old, young, rich, poor. He was interested in and at ease with anyone.

'Dad's name? Dominic Delmaestro. And Mum's is Maria. I was Sophia Delmaestro when I met Michael. We're very strong family people. Dad came from Naples province in Italy, one of eight children. He went to grade 5, then worked growing tobacco and came out when he was twenty-six. All of the eight children but one came here. My mother went to grade 3. She and Dad were married by proxy, and when she was twenty-one she came out. Dad had gone straight to a country town near Kyabram. After a while he built up a tomato-and-beef farm. I was born there. We used to be called "dagoes" at school, but the Asians are getting it now. Dad's been here for forty-five years and Mum for forty-two.'

Michael, the eldest of four children, was born in Croydon. His family was Irish Australian, Catholic-born but not practising. He finished form 5 and from then on always held a job while he studied part-time for a diploma in engineering. Sophia was employed full-time as a computer programmer.

'We got married in January 1989, a big Italian wedding, 329 guests, and 37 in the shade.' Sophia hesitates again, then asks in her well-articulated voice, 'Would you like to see the wedding pictures?'

When I open the white brocade-bound book, the reality of Sophia's loss flows out. Here a picture of a radiant mischievous Sophia in a cirrus cloud of wedding lace and tulle, sitting in the centre of her parents' bed, one shapely leg raised high as she pulls on a blue garter. Above the back of the double bed an old print of Jesus Christ mutely tells of the family's heritage. Here a picture of four rose-taffeta bridesmaids fussing with the bridal veil. Here a picture of the fair-haired groom, a strapping six foot one in the old language, two gold hoop earrings in his left ear and a smile that fills out his strong face. And here the formal portrait of the thirteen-member bridal group. Posed under a drooping willow tree, some sit on the lush green grass, others stand. A river, blue and serene, sweeps by in the background, the bride and groom look straight at the camera, faces heavy with love and sweet anticipation of the years ahead.

'We loved our life together,' Sophia tells me. 'We loved going shopping together, driving together. Michael loved sports, especially cricket. I'd do my crafts—calligraphy, cross-stitch, dry flower arrangements. We wanted a baby, and when Andrew was born some three years later we were beside ourselves with joy. At about the same time my office wanted to downsize so I took a retrenchment package. We decided not to pay off the house mortgage, but thought of going on a big holiday, of spending it on other things. We wanted another baby, and all during this time I was trying to get pregnant again.'

In May 1995, six years after their marriage, Sophia felt a sudden desire to pay the mortgage off. The feeling they should do so came out of the blue. Its vehemence surprised her.

'I was very clear about it,' she says. '"Let's not spend it," I said. "Let's pay the mortgage off now." There was absolutely no doubt in my mind this was the thing to do.'

A couple of weeks later Michael showed Sophia a small lump under his left eye. Sophia thought it might be a good idea to check it out, and about a week later they saw their GP. He thought the lump might be a blocked tear duct or a fatty deposit but felt a specialist should take a look. Neither Michael nor Sophia felt any urgency. They saw a specialist in June, and when Sophia rang him two days after he had done some tests, she had no concerns. She took it for granted that the lump was probably a fatty deposit. She couldn't believe it when he said it was a tumour and that Michael would need more tests. They'd never questioned the abundance of their life, health, future. The doctor's words wouldn't sink in. Then Sophia began to think about Michael's fair hair and skin and the way he burned badly, the skin ruddy and sometimes peeling, especially during cricket season.

A few days later the specialist told them the tumour was malignant, a melanoma. Within a month Michael had surgery at Valley Private Hospital and all glands were removed from the left side of his face. This was disfiguring but further plastic surgery restored a near normal appearance, except for a droop in the left eye.

'We didn't care about that,' Sophia says. 'He was clear of cancer and that's all that mattered. Then to our joy, after we'd been trying for eleven months, I became pregnant again. I had morning sickness for fourteen weeks. I lay on the couch all day, but thinking it was the best thing that could have happened to us. The mortgage was paid off, we had money in the bank, Andrew was healthy, everything was rosy. And then, in October the cancer came back. It had never left. We just didn't realise what a bastard melanoma is. Michael started a course of chemotherapy. He'd go to work the next day. It didn't seem to affect him.

'I remember the doctor saying about then, "It's a vicious cancer you've got. We don't know how it will affect you." I was three months pregnant and asked, "Is he going to be around for the birth?" He replied, "I can't tell you that." Michael Leung was his name. He was Asian and just excellent. I really felt good about him and was grateful for his frankness. He kept taking scans and tests. One day he showed us some X-rays and commented, "It's in Michael's bloodstream." He didn't say, "The cancer's back." Just, "It's in your bloodstream." I asked, "Will it kill him?" He said, "Most likely."

'That night we didn't sleep a wink. We held each other all night. I thought, Oh, God, don't let me lose him. That first night was terrible, but Michael bit the bullet. "I'm planning on surviving," he said. He accepted that he had cancer but not that he would die, because cancer can be beaten. He kept on working, finished his studies and went to his graduation. His face was somewhat disfigured, but it didn't stop him. He'd always been terribly energetic, was always a good dresser, ambitious, and he was determined to beat it.'

In January Michael started having back pain. He found movement painful and ordinary tasks getting beyond him. He kept working—he refused to give up.

'It was his birthday that month, his thirtieth,' Sophia continues. 'He'd always wanted a new set of golf clubs—he'd always had second-hand ones—and people were terribly generous and raised $1,300. He used to look at them and say, "I can't wait," but he never got to use them. They're sitting in the garage locked up and I haven't looked at them yet.

'In early March Michael experienced pain in his neck. The doctor said the cancer had spread there. "You can't drive any more," he said, and Michael gave up working. I was six months pregnant then, but I can't remember being pregnant. It's all a blur. I stopped going to prenatal classes. Michael needed me all the time. It took him half an hour to get out of bed. He still believed he could beat it. If people asked me what was going on, I'd tell them, but Michael didn't want any sympathy. He told me, "If anyone comes in here and says how sorry they are, I'll tell them to get out."

'I was frantic about the baby. It was due on April 19 and I kept thinking, Oh, God, let him see it, but I could see what was happening to him. I asked the doctor again, "Will he live to see the baby?" He just shook his head and said, "I can't say." Michael was in the Alfred Hospital for a week, getting radiotherapy, two beds, two patients, jammed side by side in the cancer ward. The atmosphere was awful, crowded, noisy. The melanoma had metastasised everywhere, spine, lung, skull.'

Sophia's sister, married to a farmer near Sale, came to help her, as did their mother. Eight months after Michael had noticed 'the fatty deposit', the end was now clear to everyone.

'I wanted him to do a video for the children,' Sophia informs me, 'but he couldn't bring himself to do it. Even a letter for Andrew when he was ten, then fifteen, but he couldn't. It would have been easy when he was well—you can do anything when you're well—but then he started to lose his right side and it was hard to write. I desperately wanted something to give to Andrew. I suggested Michael make a video. "What'll I say?" he asked. "Hello, I'm your Dad. I love you?" He just couldn't bring himself to do it.'

For some weeks Michael had done well with palliative care at home, but as he grew weaker the problems associated with showering, hygiene and pain control led to their agreement that he go to McCulloch House.

'Michael was really happy there. Phillip—do you know the nurses Phillip and John?—well, Phillip would organise pizza, and John would bring out a few beers, and they'd sit up till late at night playing cards in the lounge. John used to fool around a lot, and he and Michael really hit it off, had lots of laughs. Michael looked so well, he got his appetite back, I couldn't believe he was dying. I asked Peter Martin [the doctor] if there was any chance. Peter replied, "Do *you* think there's any chance?" And I knew there wasn't.'

Michael was in McCulloch House at the end of March when Sophia went to Valley Private Hospital in Mulgrave for a prenatal checkup. The baby was due in three weeks, 19 April, but it was touch-and-go whether Michael would live that long. At the hospital Sophia ran into a nurse who'd been with her when Andrew was born. This nurse wondered why Sophia couldn't have a caesarean. She suggested Sophia talk it over with Michael and get back to her. Within two days Valley Hospital and McCulloch House had it organised.

'I went into hospital on April 1, and Michael was transferred there from McCulloch House in a wheelchair taxi the next day. They had to use a harness to lift him. There was a bottle of champagne waiting for us in a lovely room. Michael had some and I had a sip. We had that night together. I was close to giving birth and he was dying. There's not much more I can say than that.'

The next day Michael sat in a wheelchair next to the operating table during the caesarean. It took a long time and Michael was very weak.

'If I'd gone into labour, he couldn't have coped. When Jonathan was handed to him, he could hardly hold him. When I saw Jonathan in Michael's arms, and Michael looked up at me, my heart almost leapt out of my chest in triumph. I did it. I made it. I felt so triumphant, and tired enough to die. Michael stayed there with me for two days. I was there a week over Easter. So many people came to the hospital to see me on Good Friday. I was a wreck. All I could do was cry. I couldn't nurse Jonathan. I was just too tired.'

When Michael returned to his room at McCulloch House, he found the staff had decorated it with balloons and blue ribbons, and he, John, and other nurses and patients had a party.

'Michael never talked about dying. He never spoke of or suggested euthanasia. He didn't have any religion. He had a fighting spirit, real courage. "I'm not going to give up," he told me. But on Thursday night when his sister Sally visited him, Michael knew it was nearly over. He gave his niece the biggest, longest hug, and I knew he knew. Friday was the 19th, the day Jonathan had been due, and I kept thinking, please, please don't die this day. I asked a nurse how long. "Probably two weeks," she said. But as soon as I arrived that evening, Peter [Martin] came over and said Michael's blood pressure had dropped. I asked him how long and he said probably a matter of hours. My brother John was a great mate of Michael's. He was there with me.

'Michael knew he was dying. That was the scary part. He was having problems breathing. I tried to help him breathe. He knew everything I was saying. His eyes were on my face. He started to haemorrhage. The staff kept wetting him down, putting cold towels on his body. He knew everything that was happening and his mind was perfectly clear. His eyes were wide open and, looking at me, he said clearly, "I'm burning up." He kept on looking, but I knew he was gone. It was Saturday morning, April 20.'

Although Michael had never spoken to Sophia of dying, he had spoken of it to a nurse and said he didn't want cremation. Over five hundred people attended his funeral, and his cricket team formed a guard of honour with cricket bats.

'Michael had patience. He never held a grudge. But I was so angry with God. At night when the baby would cry I'd weep and think, God, why have you done this? All I want now is for my children to do well. I suppose they'll get drunk sometimes and all that stuff, but they'll have nice friends. I just want them to grow up and have their dad be proud of them.'

During Michael's illness and death, Sophia learned of the abhorrence with which some people regard sickness, death, and dying. She felt strongly that Michael's family hadn't visited enough, supported her enough. Even some longtime friends withdrew. She felt betrayed and confused by this distancing. The hurt was terrible.

'Death changes people,' she now says. 'Michael's father, Tom, was sick when Michael was sick and died two weeks after him. So I know his family was coping with two deaths. We used to visit Michael's family all the time, every Sunday for dinner but they've distanced themselves since Michael died. I don't know why. They probably think I'm coping all right, but they don't see me at night when the kids are asleep and I'm in tears.

'A lot of people don't like seeing attention going to others. One relative actually said to me, "I'm jealous of all the attention you're getting." Michael was dying and she was jealous of me!' For a moment Sophia's calm voice chokes up. 'We copped so much rubbish from relatives whereas strangers were wonderful.

'When I think of Michael at McCulloch House, I remember him with his two sons on his bed, and him playing cards with John and Phillip. He didn't have the strength to deal a hand at the end, but he still won, and he still loved winning. Things like that don't change. Even if you're dying, you're still who you are. I hadn't known you could be dying but still enjoy things—still laugh, fool around, have a good appetite and enjoy your meals like Michael did. Michael never felt sorry for himself and he never gave up. I know that we were meant to be together, that I was meant to go through this with him.

'We've just gotten through the first anniversary. I keep busy, do the garden, and have set up an office at home where I work two days a week processing a payroll account. I've met someone who is three years down the track after losing his wife. She died of bowel cancer after five weeks, although she'd been "given" six months. It's early days yet. But it's boosted my friend up. We met in a support group for young people who've lost partners. He just asked me out. He had a function somewhere and needed a partner.' Then she says with surprise, as if she had forgotten, 'It was *so* nice to go out.'

Our conversation consumes an entire afternoon. I phone for a taxi and, as we wait, Sophia shows me through her spotless home. The light is fading. Outside a chill late-May wind blows. Framed in the doorway, sturdy Andrew tugging at her beige slacks and an equally solid Jonathan wriggling in her arms, Sophia looks very alone.

'Yes, and I hate being alone,' she tells me, filling her lungs with fresh air and gently stretching. 'I've gotten through this year. I haven't put the sympathy cards away yet. Maybe soon. Maybe this coming year won't be so bad.'

Palliative-care workers not only take care of people but care for people. Sitting at the long polished table in the quiet McCulloch House lounge, with the weak wintry sun now fading and the evening visitors yet to arrive, I talk with thirty-one-year-old John. He is a sturdy energetic man, a gentle nurse, spontaneous in speech, and given to a slightly offbeat humour that irritates a couple of his co-workers but which makes him highly popular with patients, to whom he is devoted. He is musically gifted but untrained. He has played the piano by ear since he was four, and after hearing a piece can often reproduce it. People associate music with specific events in their lives, and patients often ask John to play old favourites they have no other way of hearing.

'No one touched me like Michael Fulton,' he tells me. 'We'd drink beer, play cards, eat chips, fool around, joke. When you're with someone like that, they become different, become important to you. You're doing everything for them, they trust you, all the macho bullshit between men is gone. They're dying and it's hurting you like hell that they're dying. That's the way it was with Michael, and I'll never forget him. When he went, it was very hard.

'This isn't like ordinary nursing, with a crowded ward and a big staff turnover and different assignments. Here you get to really nurse a patient in an old-fashioned, hands-on way, to do everything for them, to care for them as if you were one of their family. Michael knew that it was hard on me. That might sound funny to you, but in palliative care you sort of offer yourself to the patient. You let them see your feelings, too, and this can give them a lot of strength.

'I'd never thought of being a nurse. I grew up in Casterton fifty kilometres from Mount Gambier. I left school at sixteen, wasn't very good at it. Tertiary education was never thought of in my family and I was never encouraged academically. You grew up, married, had children, that was it. I don't feel any resentment about that. I fell into a job at the local bank, stayed, transferred to a Ballarat bank for five years, then on to Avoca in the Victorian Pyrenees, a wine-growing area. When I was in Ballarat, I went to the Australian Catholic University and found to my surprise I was quite bright. Still didn't know what I wanted to do but finally did a three-year degree in nursing. The whole time I trained I hated it. All the old hands-on nurses treated us badly.

'I went to St Vincent's Hospital for twelve months and decided I couldn't stand acute nursing. We were so busy I hardly touched a patient the whole time I was there. I remember sitting down talking to a patient one day and one of the nurses told me off. I needed to make a difference in someone's life, to be acknowledged as having something more than a tablet to offer. The director of nursing suggested I have a look at Caritas Christi, a hospital for the terminally ill. I stayed a year and found it fascinating and then came here to McCulloch House.

'My big discovery was that death is nothing to be frightened of. You can just be talking to someone and they die. Or someone will ask, "Why can't I die?" And you can just sit with them and let them talk, and you might make a joke about it assuring them that they will, and both of you end up laughing. There's nothing like laughter. That's what I love about McCulloch House. People here, staff too, are allowed to be individuals, so it's more like the wacky world of the outside. If people want their morphine at seven instead of eight o'clock, they can have it. If they want wine or whisky with their lunch as well as at night, they can have it. We want them to feel they're at home and able to have the same things they'd have at home.

'In many hospitals nurses act as if they own the patient. They march into their rooms without knocking, strip the patient down to bathe without considering their modesty and entirely at their own convenience. Here we knock on the door, wash patients when they want to be washed. We're aware it might be humiliating. Can you imagine what it must be like to have a stranger barging into your bathroom or stripping you naked?

'I'm a very restless type of person. I'm single, I live in a flat, and every year I move to a different suburb. I like sampling suburbs the way some people like sampling special dishes. I like to spread the idea that being in palliative care isn't like being in a library, everyone tippy-toe and hushed, as if everyone were dead. The sounds of life are very important. Someone said to me, "That patient is depressed because you told him all the good things you did this weekend and he can't do it." But that's bullshit. Patients want to know how my weekend went. I think it makes it easier for them to tell their own stories, and these stories often become a review of their life. They don't want to feel their life was a lot of nothing. They want to talk about it and validate it.'

John says he did a sixteen-week pastoral-care course, telling himself it would be good for the patients. But it threw his life into turmoil as he realised how badly he needed it for himself, particularly to improve his capacity to listen and reflect. Working in palliative care had opened up unknown parts within himself and helped him to be more at ease with his own feelings, and less frightened to reveal them.

'Since I've been here, I make the most of my time off. I tend not to put things off. If you want to go on a holiday, go. Do it. If you want something and can afford it, buy it. If you love someone, tell them. You're dead a long time.'

When a medical system such as palliative care rejects a hierarchical structure and empowers all those who work in it, suffering can be ameliorated even in the worst cases. Had palliative care not been accessible to Michael, had he spent his last weeks in an acute-care hospital, he would have been denied almost everything that made the last few weeks of his life worth living. What if a creative nurse hadn't suggested a caesarean delivery? If McCulloch House hadn't co-operated? If Sophia had given birth, separated from Michael, on the day he died? If Michael hadn't lived to see and hold the new baby? How different would the years ahead have been for Sophia and her family? How much more at peace is she today, how much more self-reliant and capable of good parenting, because creative responses to the needs of the dying had the freedom to be enacted?

For Sophia and Michael Fulton hope provided a strength that enabled them to cope. In the initial stages of Michael's illness they hoped for a complete recovery. Believing all cancer had been removed, Michael and Sophia kept trying for another child. When more evidence of cancer was found, Michael voiced his will to defeat it. He expressed both courage and hope by continuing to work, to study, and to graduate. As his condition weakened, the object of his hope changed.

Michael no doubt realised he was dying. His refusal to discuss it with Sophia was his way of fostering hope, not for a future together but for Sophia and his children. By fostering hope he kept the destructive effects of despair at a distance. His articulated determination to recover was the best way for him, and a pregnant Sophia, to handle the painfully unreal situation in which they found themselves. Sophia could voice her needs—for Michael to write his children a letter or make a video—but for Michael to do so would have been to acknowledge his death. His heartbreaking inability to accede to Sophia's wishes reflects not only his awareness of his approaching end but the fact it would create a sort of official validation of death that would destroy all hope and create despair.

Sophia, a sensible intelligent woman, knew Michael could not recover, but hope kept her going—the hope that Michael would live to see their new child. Sophia knew that if Michael died without holding the child they had tried so long to create, she would feel that pain for the rest of her life. She intuitively understood that the hope he expressed—'I'm not giving up'—

was directed at first to his own life, but then, in the face of medical reality, to the approaching birth of his child and the future of his children.

These expressions of hope kept both of them going, helped Sophia deliver safely and helped Michael see his new son. Although Sophia had delivered her baby, it was no coincidence that Michael's body gave up one day after the baby's normal due date. 'Hanging on' for a particular event, such as an anniversary or Christmas, is, as all health professionals know, a widely recognised phenomenon among the terminally ill.

The happy atmosphere at McCulloch House nurtured and supported this sense of hope. The card games with John and Phillip, the chips, beer, the jokes and fooling around, all allowed Michael's humanity free play. Hope played a powerful role in the nurse who suggested Sophia have a caesarean, and in the actions of Valley Private Hospital and McCulloch House staff who made it happen. Hope was manifested in the blue streamers and balloons that decorated Michael's room after Jonathan's delivery, a hope for Michael whose life would continue in his children.

An image strikes me—of McCulloch House opening its doors wide to hope, allowing hope full freedom to circulate down the corridors and into the rooms, touching patients and staff alike with the lightness and freshness of air. With this imagery comes a slight but unsettling intimation that hope can carry a meaning beyond what is obvious. Intimidating, because what can that meaning be? Hope is the most human impulse. It needs no further dimension. Yet it clearly has one strong enough to allow full life until death.

That night, after visiting Sophia, I go to sleep thinking it a pity that the things that nourish our spirit are usually excluded from our short-staffed busy hospitals, where the terminally ill simply wait for the end in wards that are little more than warehouses for the dying. Why do we put up with it? I wonder. We, who are so fussy about reading good books, seeing good movies, buying healthy, interesting food. Why are we willing to take the chance we will die like an unloved dog?

# Denial

*We can believe what we choose. We are answerable for what we choose to believe.*

—Cardinal Newman, from a letter to Mrs William Froude

We can't act with our full human powers and dignity if we are plagued by severe chronic pain or discomfort. Severe pain can make it impossible to sit, move, talk, or even think. Even moderate pain that follows a voluntary act, such as stretching one's arm, can discourage us from attempting any activity. Severe pain can also prevent us from understanding the implications of a proposed treatment or procedure. If we cannot exercise the right to make a decision for ourselves, we are disempowered at a most crucial time of our life. As for maintaining dignity, that is virtually impossible if one is suffering intense pain. And just when we need moral strength the most, a pain-soaked consciousness can block the messages of love and support from others that help validate our lives.

Psychological and spiritual pain can also overwhelm us, creating as 'bad' a death as can physical pain. Unlike physical pain, which pharmacology and treatment techniques can generally control, psychological and spiritual pain can be beyond anyone's power to ameliorate. It is subtle, often deeply rooted, and highly individual. If you go through life keeping your thoughts and feelings to yourself, and rarely, if ever, give them voice, you will likely die in the same way. Even if you attempt to reach out and express what you now find demands expression, you may be unable to do so. Even an acutely sensitive caregiver, open to your suffering and wanting to help you, won't be able to guess what is on your mind and will be able to do little more than offer low-key everyday comfort.

The process of dying is only a small part of our entire life. Although a critical time, it is still but a moment in a lifetime during which we established our own individual habits, attitudes, values and standards. These characteristics do not automatically dissipate because we are dying. On the contrary, they can powerfully assert themselves.

Every day at McCulloch House I visit any patient who feels inclined to spend a few minutes with me. The majority of people appear to accept their approaching death with resignation, calm, and even serenity. Many, perhaps without any formal or religious upbringing or language, experience the dying process as a time of spiritual growth and awakening. Sometimes when one of them makes a simple remark, they choose words that are unconsciously metaphorical. 'I had a wonderful dream last night,' one woman tells me. 'I was swimming when a huge, salty wave rolled in and carried me to shore.' Another woman, raised in a traditional religion, tells me she 'slept like an angel'. One man remarks how short the days are becoming and how quickly night is falling.

From these daily visits I learn how we can help to create a good or bad death for ourselves. If we live our lives as if they have no ending, as if our supply of life is unlimited, if we believe the power, strength and beauty of our youth and middle age are set in stone and constitute who we really are and always will be, we are helping to create a bad death for ourselves. We die in the same spirit in which we have lived. If we have been aware of our life's passage, of the different seasons of our soul, and have been open to accepting the unexpected in life, we will likely enter into the dying process with a sense of the totality of life, that we have arrived on time at the end which, unknown to us, awaited us from our birth.

Some of us, however, mentally create a private and detailed program of exactly how our life should, and will, unfold. We assume it is a matter of willpower and intelligence to realise that program and we suffer profoundly if an illness such as cancer arbitrarily interferes and ultimately destroys it. If we cannot let go of the sense of entitlement to that life that we see stretching into the future, but which, in fact, is about to end, we die bitterly. This is particularly true of lives that have been based on the assumption that we were put on this planet to make money. 'Why me?' is the commonest question asked by such patients.

Such a case is Graham Davey, a successful forty-six-year-old businessman, owner of a winter condo at Noosa Heads and, with his wife, a frequent international traveller. He has three children, two sons, twenty-two and nineteen, and a daughter, fifteen. He was diagnosed six months ago with stomach cancer, which has subsequently spread to his liver.

I meet Graham one sunny afternoon, sitting in a wheelchair on the tiled verandah by the new garden. He was at McCulloch House for a respite stay two weeks earlier, returning home after his medication was adjusted and level of comfort improved. The day before, however, he was brought back to McCulloch

House, clearly for the last time. He seems comfortable enough on this day, watching nothing in particular, a light blanket over his long skeletal legs. Initially he isn't much interested in talking. He looks at me in the invisible way younger men look at older women, but brightens slightly when I start talking about sports.

Graham isn't a person I feel instantly comfortable with. His rare laughter comes in short, sharp bites, and his tendency to speak dismissively to the nurses indicates a man essentially ill at ease with women. I imagine in his normal life this aspect of his personality was well controlled, emerging only in sexist jokes or in the way he promoted within his company. Fatigue, pain, and bitterness at fate have worn down his ability to disguise himself, however, and what is eventually revealed is a man in profound psychological pain.

When I see Graham again I ask him about his willingness to be interviewed. He says he will think about it. The next day there is a note at the front desk asking me to stop by his room. He will agree to participate in my interviews only if his and his family's names aren't used. We finally settle on the name Graham Davey, Joanne for his wife, Nicholas, Bruce, and Zara for his children. This exercise breaks the ice a little, and over the course of two days he tells his story. (With Graham's story I have included the names of the drugs used in treating him to provide general pharmacological information that will not be repeated in other narratives.)

He was the youngest of three boys raised on a small Gippsland dairy farm, not far from Bairnsdale. He was born three years after his father returned from fighting in North Africa and New Guinea in World War II. His mother had kept the farm going, milking twenty cows twice a day.

'She'd been the local schoolteacher, for all the good it did her,' he says. 'Much better educated than Dad. They met at a dance in the local hall. Last thing she wanted was to be an old maid, I suppose.'

Graham thinks his mother was fair, but he doesn't have a good word to say about his father. His mother excused the father, saying the war had changed him. 'Always making excuses for the old bugger' is how Graham describes it. 'I remember she yelled at him once that she wished he was back in New Guinea, that she'd been better off without him. He looked like she'd whacked him with a fence post. Anyway, they stuck it out, like people did then.'

At sixteen Graham took off for Melbourne. When he told his mother his plans, she produced a jar from under her bed and gave him money that paid for his train fare and a week's lodging at a Carlton boarding house. By the end of that week, Graham had a job loading goods for a trucking company. One of the customers was a sporting-goods store in Chapel Street, Prahran. Graham soon had a job there, carrying boxes and loading shelves, eventually moving behind the counter.

'Never had a penny to my name at home. Was used to going without, cutting corners. I stayed on in that lousy boarding house, stinking of grease and the toilet at the end of the hall. Saved every penny and kept my eyes open. My old man said I was too big for my britches, that life'd cut me down to size. Like it had him, I suppose. Good for me he was such a mean bastard. Made me want to show him, make money, shove it in his face.'

A fellow clerk in the store taught him tennis, and he turned out to be pretty good at it. He started playing in Saturday afternoon matches at Kew, where he met Joanne. He was twenty-one at the time, Joanne eighteen. They went out together for four years before marrying. Finally he found a small shop at the top end of Glenferrie Road, on the tram line and not too far from the train station.

When he tells me about that first shop, he gives a short bark of a laugh and says, 'Dusty, fly-spotted windows, filthy. But I could see its potential. I made money, eventually sold it and moved into real estate development and never looked back.'

'Any other financial interests?' I ask.

'Nosy, aren't we? Yeah, there are. A twenty-unit building at Surfers, a restaurant, a small part of a factory in China. I've got to dump that. It's too much of a headache. And I got smart on the stock market. That satisfy you?'

Memories of his youth have revitalised him. The excitement, challenges, thrill of making money, of winning a game to which he attaches prestige and importance have momentarily returned and lifted him out of the nightmarish present. Now he sinks into his pillows, his gaunt face pinched and grey. He lifts a thin arm, pounds the bedcover, and curses. Cancer is the enemy. Cancer is the bastard thief robbing him of everything he has spent his life accumulating.

The following day he is in a wretched mood. But telling his story is one unfinished business he has the power to complete. He has spent time overnight thinking about his life, because his first words to me are: 'Running, I was always running.'

'You wanted to be a success,' I remind him.

He doesn't reply. Finally, with great intensity he says, 'I just didn't want to be another bloody farmer, that's what. My brothers, they loved it. Takes all sorts. Both still live in Bairnsdale, kept the farm, have it as a hobby.' He shakes his head in disgust, lost in the past, then for a few minutes he is lost in sleep. His dosage of morphine has been increased from thirty milligrams every four hours to forty and his body is still adjusting.

When Graham awakes, he is sharp and lucid. He starts by

saying sadly, 'Funny, I took it for granted I'd get old, live into my seventies at least. Mum lived to be eighty-two, Dad seventy-four. All these advances in medicine aren't doing me much good, are they?' Even though he laughs, he looks as if he wants to cry. Awareness of my inability to say anything, do anything, to assuage it leaves me sick and silent.

Gradually, in brusque sentences, his face set like rock, he describes the course of his illness. I ask for access to his current medical records, which he reluctantly allows. An interview with Joanne fills out sufficient details to gain a general overview of the past six months of his life.

Graham says that at forty-five he felt life spreading before him into an unlimited horizon. He was careful to stay in top form. He worked out two nights a week under a personal trainer, and often played doubles tennis on Saturday with Joanne and business associates. The only indulgence he allowed himself was a half-bottle of red wine a night. Sundays he usually spent locked in his office at home reviewing the week's business and planning his next acquisition. He had an office set up in their Noosa condo, which Joanne didn't like, but then, as Graham points out, 'She didn't make the money, did she?' This way he could maintain control of his head office from a distance.

Six months earlier he had attended a real estate developers' convention in San Francisco. He had gone rather than send someone because he felt he needed a break. His appetite was off, and San Francisco had great food. Besides, Joanne had been getting on his nerves, telling him he had to slow down, going on about how he would kill himself if he didn't stop doing eighteen-hour days. 'How much money do we need?' she'd say. To Graham, this was 'one bloody joke as I made it and she spent it'. They had a row and he took off for San

Francisco. Graham said that it suited him to go and that it reminded his wife who really called the shots.

He was gone only a week, but when he returned a couple of people remarked how thin he looked. He had lost a couple of kilograms, but then he wasn't eating well. Even San Francisco hadn't helped restore his appetite. The problem was indigestion. Anything triggered it. Joanne 'nagged' him until he went to his doctor who did some simple blood tests and put him on Zantac (tanitidine), an antacid for ulcers. The doctor told Graham to come back in three or four weeks for a gastroscopy if he wasn't feeling better.

'A week after that,' Graham recalls, 'I was out to lunch with my lawyer and a couple of business associates from Queensland and I threw up. It was bloody embarrassing. I was in the middle of negotiating the building of a shopping mall on the Sunshine Coast—the biggest development they'll have there, and the biggest single project I've ever undertaken.'

'Your wife must have felt worried, you throwing up like that,' I say.

The unending scope of Graham's ambitions are revealing themselves, and I wonder just what their impact has been on family life. I have seen the family in the front lounge. Joanne is short and fair-haired, with the taut arms and well-shaped calves of a dedicated tennis player. She looks like an older sister to her two quiet, well-mannered sons, neither of whom have inherited their father's height but who are gifted with handsome looks and graceful bodies. Zara, at fifteen, has rebellion written all over her pretty, pouting face, untidy hair and sloppy clothes. Joanne defers to the boys, and perhaps for this reason Zara seems on the fringe of the family.

'My daughter told me I looked rotten, too,' Graham tells me, 'so I went back to my GP. He said I probably had a peptic ulcer and set up a gastroscopy. I thought it a damn nuisance in the middle of this deal. I didn't have time for all this messing about.'

To Graham's irritation, the doctor told him to bring his wife. He would be given a tranquilliser for the procedure and would have to be driven home. After twenty-three years of marriage, this was the first time Graham had allowed her to drive him. Joanne later described it as the beginning of a huge change in their relationship.

Graham went on, 'After the gastroscopy I asked the nurse for the results. But the old cow got cagey and said the gastro-enterologist would be in touch. As I was leaving, I ran into him in the corridor. He just smiled hello and walked on, but I went after him and asked what he'd found. He said all the results would be sent immediately to my GP, who'd discuss it with me the next day. I felt so damn mad. Here I was in the middle of these negotiations. I couldn't take another bloody day off. But I just said, "Right, I'll call him tomorrow."'

That night Graham couldn't sleep. He asked Joanne to accompany him the next day, a request that surprised her because it was very unlike Graham to ask her for any support. At the doctor's office the nurse called him in, but the doctor, rising from behind his desk, said it would be a good idea to bring Joanne in as well.

The doctor got right to the point. 'I have some bad news about the test yesterday.'

'What?' Graham demanded. 'Tell me. I've got a bad ulcer?'

'No, it's a little worse than that.'

'What do you mean?' Graham asked as Joanne placed her hand on his arm. He jerked away from her hand impatiently. 'What is it?'

The doctor hesitated. 'What would you be frightened of finding out?'

'Cancer.'

'I'm afraid that's what it is. You've got stomach cancer.'

To me, Graham says, 'I remembered nothing after that. Later Joanne told me what the doctor said. She said he had a really hard time trying to be honest. I kept shouting at him—honest to God I don't remember doing that—saying I couldn't possibly have cancer, I was only forty-five. I had this big deal in the works. It really pissed me off. No one, no one seemed to understand what it takes to get a deal like this going, and here they were telling me I had cancer.'

The doctor said he would set up appointments for Graham to see a surgeon one week and an oncologist the next. The doctor struggled to be positive, saying they would 'get the best deal on it'. He asked them to come back the next day to discuss the dates and times.

At that point Graham completely lost it. Bewildered, incredulous, he shouted that he couldn't stop for surgery. 'I'm *it*,' he cried. 'I'm the boss, the owner, the head honcho. There's nobody to take my place. I'm in the middle of a big deal. You told me it was indigestion. Three weeks ago you said indigestion. Now you say it's bloody cancer.'

The following day, unknown to Graham, Joanne called their doctor back, saying she wanted to see him alone. During this meeting she told the doctor her father had suffered from lung cancer and she had helped her mother nurse him at home until he had died. She feared the same death for her husband and didn't feel she could handle it. She said the children called their father 'a control freak', and it was true that he liked everything done his way. He had provided very well for his family and felt that put him 'in charge of us all'.

When the doctor asked about Graham's relationship with his children, Joanne burst into tears. She said that the oldest boy, Nicholas, had finished his degree in commerce, worked for his father, but hated it because Graham still treated him as if he were a child. Bruce refused to go to university and, after a fearful row with his father, had moved out. She had phoned him the night before to tell him about his father's cancer and begged him to return home. And Zara, who had been her father's pet when she was small, in the past two years had become 'awful'. Recently she had told her father he wasn't going to bully her the way he did the others, and Graham had slapped her face. Since then they had barely spoken.

The doctor suggested that Joanne might want to consider consulting with a psychologist or social worker, just for support, and Joanne said she might think about it. But she knew Graham would hit the roof if she did something like that.

A week later Graham was seen by a surgeon. According to Joanne, 'he was about Graham's age and just full of himself. His manner was really offhand. We felt totally overwhelmed, still couldn't believe it. We did grasp that the only option was to remove part or the whole of the stomach.'

The surgeon ordered a histology, a microscopic study of tissue, to find out what kind of cancer Graham had and how well differentiated it was. The information, with a diagram, was faxed to the GP. The diagram showed a six-centimetre tumour on the lesser curve of the stomach. The notes ended: 'Histology x 2. Pretty horrible, poor prognosis.'

Two days later Bruce and Joanne visited the oncologist, who was cautious and answered every question with, 'We'll just have to wait and see what surgery reveals.' The oncologist was struck by Graham's impatience and that he twice mentioned his schedule couldn't be cancelled 'for anything'. The doctor tried to confront Graham with how serious his condition was. Finally he told him, 'Maybe we'll give you some chemotherapy, but again, let's wait and see what the surgery shows. In the meantime we need a scan of the liver, so we'll set that up.'

In the lounge of McCulloch House after Graham's death, Joanne describes her husband's reaction to this news. 'Graham just blew up again at that. I think by then I knew how serious it was, although I had no idea that stomach cancer was so aggressive. But Graham just couldn't take it in. At this stage it wasn't fear but rage that his plans were thwarted. He'd have to miss work, change his schedules. All he saw in life was his work. He was blind to the fact that his life was ending.'

She pauses, then says, 'All the signs were there of something really wrong. He'd lost about six kilos by then, was nauseated on and off, going to the toilet a lot, throwing up. I'd always enjoyed getting him good meals—sometimes I felt food and sex were the only communication we had—but now he wouldn't eat and he wasn't interested in sex. It was as if he became afraid of it, as if it might harm him.'

Sighing deeply, she continues. 'Anyway, he went in for an abdominal ultrasound. Our GP told me they were looking for liver metastases, but I didn't tell Graham that. He'd had to fast for six hours, hadn't had his morning coffee and was like a bomb ready to explode. When the technician wouldn't tell him the results, he blew up, saying he was working and didn't have time to waste. So he phoned up our GP and blasted him about the lousy system. "Don't you know what it's like to have to wait twenty-four hours for results?" he said. "I've got to know what's happening. Everything at work is on hold, and my managers are waiting to arrange our conference." It made me sick to hear how he was going on, but it was just another way he had of exercising control.'

The ultrasound indicated no evidence of cancer in the liver, that it was confined to the stomach. Two days later Graham entered hospital for surgery. On arrival he was angry and embarrassed to receive a big 'best wishes' card from his office. He hated that: it made him feel written off.

Surgeons performed a partial gastrectomy and removed a few lymph nodes that seemed to be affected by the cancer. He was given a blood transfusion, and after a few days was allowed a little water. A week later he could eat a small meal, and eleven days after the operation he was back home.

He still had no appetite and couldn't get back the weight he had lost, but on the whole he felt better. Despite Joanne's heated protests he went back to work after three weeks. He thought he was going to recover.

When his energy didn't pick up, Graham checked in with his oncologist, who offered him palliative chemotherapy. Characteristically Graham demanded to know 'what the hell' it was. After a moment's hesitation the oncologist cautiously told him the chemotherapy would make him feel better, that it would keep the cancer under control.

For six weeks Graham went once a week to the Oncology Day Centre at Monash Medical Centre where he received a drip of 5 fluorouracil (an anticancer drug) and folinic acid. The cancer was incurable, and this was simply an attempt to help him keep going a little while longer. But no one told him that.

Graham kept losing weight and lost interest in sex entirely. He was tired and irritable and complained that the pain he had now and again was becoming continuous. He had bought Panadeine from the chemist, but it made him constipated and he was reluctant to take it. He still insisted on going into the office, and although Joanne urged him to sit down with her and talk the situation over with the children, he refused. He was adamant that he was OK, claiming the chemotherapy would do the trick.

But his weight loss persisted, as did his fatigue and frustration. Ten weeks after the original diagnosis, Graham had lost ten kilograms. His oncologist noted that he looked a little anaemic. Pressing the right-hand side of Graham's rib cage, he discovered some tenderness and scheduled another ultrasound.

'I went with Graham for the results,' Joanne says. 'The oncologist was very blunt. He simply said that the ultrasound showed metastases in the liver. I knew what that meant but Graham didn't have a clue. He only paid attention to things he could make use of. "It means it's spread, that you have five different spots on the liver," the oncologist said.'

Joanne sighs and tells me that only then did the real situation begin to dawn on Graham. 'He was angry and frightened. He raised his voice. "Why didn't you tell me? I thought I was getting better. For God's sake, are you trying to tell me…are you trying to tell me…?" Then the specialist looked right at him and said, "Have you put your affairs in order?" When we got down to the car, I drove and Graham didn't say a word. He was numb with shock and rage.

'Over the next two weeks he hardly spoke. He was tired, weak, couldn't eat, and the ache in his stomach was now a real bother. The oncologist had given him a script for Panadeine Forte to be taken every six hours. As well, he was taking Metoclopramide for his nausea, and something for constipation. The oncologist had said he didn't think more chemo would be any help, and yet Graham still called the office and said he wouldn't be back for "a few more days". He still hadn't told his managers anything!'

When the GP dropped by and suggested Graham might need to go on morphine, he flatly refused, claiming he didn't want to get addicted, that the whole idea scared the hell out of him. It was as if Graham interpreted the doctor's suggestion as meaning he would die soon, or worse, that the morphine would be given to him, he would lose all control, and would die comatose and unaware.

In the days that followed Graham's pain increased, as did his anger. 'Why didn't you tell me I was going down the tube?' he shouted during one visit from his GP.

Joanne shouted back, 'Don't say that! Stop it!'

'It's the truth, the bloody truth. How long? Tell me how long?'

'Months, maybe even weeks,' the doctor said. 'We can do a lot to help the pain. You'll need to go on morphine, just a small amount, ten milligrams twice a day. I'll leave the script behind.'

'For two days,' Joanne recalls, 'the script sat on the bedroom table. But then the pain got so bad I went and got it filled. The pain went almost entirely. Then his bowels wouldn't work, but we got a new medication and that came good, and he continued with the anti-nausea medication. He wasn't sick any more and felt a lot better, but was very tired and losing weight all the time. Within a couple of weeks we had to up the morphine dose to twenty milligrams twice a day, and the anti-nausea dose went up to four times daily.'

Graham was devastated. 'They should have told me how sick I was,' he said when he recalled that time for me. 'They should have told me. I would have gotten us all together somehow and gone on a big, splashy holiday. All together. I, well…I'm not a total bastard, you know. Everything I did I did for them. I should have spent more time with them, but how was I to bloody well know I wasn't going to make it to fifty?

Why the hell me? Why me?'

I had no answer to that, so I simply remarked that it must have been very hard to tell his associates at work.

'Worst thing of all,' he admitted, indicating his priorities. 'I told my manager I was taking a bit of sick leave. I didn't want him coming to the house, seeing me, and talking about it back at the office. So I dictated two lots of instructions to Joanne— one for short-term decisions and one for long-term. I sent the short-term by courier to the head office and left the rest with my solicitor.'

That day he had sounded so competent, so in control. But in the McCulloch House lounge Joanne tells me, 'One day he phoned Bob, his head manager, and said he was sending in some instructions. Just before he hung up I heard him say, "No, Bob, no, mate, I won't be coming back." Then he put down the phone and cried. I was in the kitchen. It was the first time I'd ever heard him cry. I wanted to go in and put my arms around him, but I daren't. When he was well, he liked sex, but he wasn't really affectionate.'

However, Joanne says, things changed. 'He became much less aggressive, quieter, terribly sad. I could feel myself becoming more assertive and he didn't seem to mind. It's a terrible thing to say, but in one way it was almost a happy time for me, to have him dependent on me, to be able to do things my way and not have him blow up. He began saying thanks for small things I'd done all our married life and he'd never noticed before.'

'And what about the children?' I ask.

'Nicholas had always made an effort to get on with his dad. I even think he did commerce to please him. It wouldn't have been his choice. Bruce came home and made a point of spending time with his dad, which helped me a lot. Zara, well, she was quite mixed-up. She felt guilty that her dad was dying and she still didn't like him. Graham tried to talk with her, but she'd just sit there, saying nothing. The palliative-care nurse who came in daily could see what was going on with Zara and asked if I'd like the social worker to come in. But Graham said no. He wasn't keen on having strangers into our house. He wasn't a man who could share his life. The palliative-care volunteer offered to come to the house and give me a break, but neither of us wanted that. My girlfriends took turns sitting in while I did the shopping.'

In the three weeks that followed, Graham's condition rapidly declined. He could eat little more than jellies and soup, he required regular enemas that painfully embarrassed him, and as well as the dull constant ache he now had a sharp pain. The GP said that the pain was caused by the stretching of the liver capsule as the liver tumours grew. The doctor also told Graham that he had ascites—fluid retained in the abdomen—which could be drained off by a needle or by diuretics. On leaving he gave Joanne a new script for forty milligrams of long-acting, slow-release morphine, and for cortisone called Dexamethasone, a four-milligram tablet, both to be taken twice a day.

Graham continued to lose weight as his abdomen swelled with fluid. The doctor tried Lasix, then Aldactone, but both diuretics made Graham nauseous. By now he was sitting up only three to four hours a day. Reluctantly he let the palliative-care nurse assist him in showering and expressed surprise at how much easier that made it. Joanne ensured regular medication, tried to feed him, looked after every need, struggled with him back and forth to the commode chair, and fielded a stream of visitors and endless phone calls. Exhausted, she made an appointment with Sandra, the pastoral-care worker.

'I felt so guilty talking about Graham to another woman

while he was still alive,' she says. 'But I just had to tell someone how exhausted I was, how confused, and for some reason, how angry I was. It was as though all the resentment I'd stored up against Graham all our married life was ready to burst out. I knew exactly how Zara felt! That was the awful part; I understood Zara and I knew what she couldn't bear in her father, because I couldn't either.'

'What was it that you hated?' I ask.

Joanne can't stop her tears. For all her money and beauty she felt unappreciated and unloved. 'In one way we were important to him. He was proud of our home, loved giving big parties, liked me trim and well turned out. But, as persons, like separate people, we'd never really been important to him, not the way his work was. We were just *there*, just more evidence of his success, part of his acquisitions. We were the necessary backdrop to his life. He never stopped to think we had lives of our own. When he'd come home at night—those times when he did—none of us were ever asked how we'd spent our day, what we'd done, how we felt. The deals he was doing dominated everything.'

Joanne pauses, her face clouding with resentment. 'For years he let us down, not turning up for school concerts, being away during birthdays. We didn't count, not the way work counted. And I wanted to scream that at him. The poor darling, lying there dying, so sick and wretched, and I could hardly stop myself from shaking him. He'd never been a father, never been a mate to me! I worked, really worked at being what he wanted me to be. The perfect little wife, the perfect mother, the perfect hostess. And he took it all for granted, raised hell if it wasn't *exactly* as he had in mind.'

At this point Joanne can't go on. Her anger is as violent as her grief. Then, dabbing her eyes, she says, 'The pastoral-care worker helped me greatly. I couldn't have kept going without her.'

One night towards the end of his illness at home, Graham started vomiting what looked like coffee grounds. The small flecks of blood were followed by a couple of clots. He couldn't keep his Kapinol down, and as his pain increased, so did his confusion and aggression. Finally, struggling with Joanne to get to his commode, he fell to the floor. At 3 a.m. Joanne called the palliative-care nurse.

'The nurse suggested a syringe driver [a butterfly needle that is taped to the skin and injects morphine at the patient's wish]. But I couldn't see it. Graham was too muddled-up and very upset when he had pain. But when the nurse suggested palliative care, I broke down. I couldn't go on looking after him, but I thought of palliative care as the end.'

But it wasn't the end. Graham was taken by ambulance to McCulloch House the next day and his medication was adjusted. He was given forty milligrams of oxycodone (a morphine derivative) four times a day, amitryptiline as an antidepressant, and 2.5 milligrams of haloperidol to reduce the agitation caused by the increase in opioids. He was also rehydrated with subcutaneous fluids and after three days was well enough to return home.

'I was terrified of him dying at home,' Joanne remembers. 'They assured me at McCulloch House that, if things changed, he could go back in. I'd talked a fair bit with Barbara [social worker]. She was able to calm my fears about Graham dying at home. I also talked to her about Zara, and she pointed out that, even if Zara didn't like Graham, she was still a teenager experiencing death at close quarters, and the death of the only father she'd ever have. So she was suffering too. I hadn't thought of that. It didn't solve the problem, but at least my being able to see that stopped me from going on at Zara and making things worse.'

After two restless weeks at home, Graham was brought back to McCulloch House at Joanne's request. It was at that time that I met him. Despite his closeness to the end he was surprisingly energetic and alert. He was taken off haloperidol, a major tranquilliser, in case it was contributing to his restlessness, and put on a lesser tranquilliser, Clonazepam.

The last time I saw Graham was four days before his death. He was receiving fluid intravenously, a catheter was in place and 200 milligrams of morphine was subcutaneously administered every twenty-four hours. Periods of sleep were followed by periods of some agitation. Most of the agitation was a side effect from the morphine. The staff constantly monitored him for any sign of pain. When asked if he had any discomfort, Graham said no and shook his head. He was, however, a man entirely without peace. The anger, the disbelief, that had raged in him since his diagnosis had been replaced by grief thick with bitterness. There were no messages of comfort or strength for his family.

'I knew when there were gaps in his breathing he was going,' Joanne says. 'I remembered my father's death, the short gaps in breathing, the panting, the gaps between breaths getting longer. And then one breath, you wait for the next, but it never comes. His eyes were closed, his mouth was open. The children stood by his bed for a moment, then left. I sat on while they took out the catheter. The nurses gave me a hug and asked if I'd like to help wash and change him. I felt I should. But I couldn't bring myself to. Not only because I was so tired. I'd just had enough.'

'And what about Zara?' I ask.

'I'd like to say there was some sort of reconciliation. But there wasn't. I made her go and kiss her father while he was still conscious, but left alone she wouldn't have gone near him. Zara's a bit like him—hard, unsentimental. Yet, funnily enough, in the month Graham's been gone we've been getting on better together. I know she despised me for accepting the crap Graham dished out. The boys understood but Zara didn't. Now he's gone, well, I can be a little more assertive, more myself.'

'In what ways?'

Joanne hesitates, uncertain how much to tell me. Then she says firmly, 'I've decided to take over Graham's business. I knew for several months Graham was going to die, realised it long before he did. I gave my future a lot of thought. I learned a lot about business from Graham, hearing him go on about it over the years. Not that he ever sought my opinion! Nicholas will work with me, and the other two children seem happy with that. In fact, when I told Zara, she shouted, "Right on!" and gave me a spontaneous hug. And Bruce has moved back home!' She looks at me, suddenly embarrassed that the lilt in the last few words might sound inappropriately triumphant.

Joanne dropped by McCulloch House on the day of our interview to see Barbara, the social worker. I felt relieved when Joanne told me why she was there. She will do well in the long run, but seems unaware of all the adjustments to be made in the months ahead. She had been with Graham as girlfriend, then wife, since she was eighteen. She is now forty-three. She was used to Graham, to his speech, his ways, his bodily presence. Now all she can feel is her freedom. Like a bird released from a cage, she is flexing her wings, unaware of the time to be passed and the work to be done before the safety and security of that cage will cease to look, in rosy retrospect, like heaven.

Most of the nurses get to know the patients at McCulloch House and one of the many who tended Graham was Phyllis, a native of County Armagh, Northern Ireland. Trained as a nurse, she married at twenty-one and eight weeks later, with her husband Pat, emigrated to Australia. In 1990 she and Pat returned to Ireland for two years with their two sons, thirteen and sixteen. Pat drove trucks all over Northern Ireland, working for a firm not known to employ Catholics. If he was in a Protestant area and it became known that his name was Pat, no one would help him unload the truck. If he was in a Catholic area, he would be stoned for driving a Protestant truck. They loved Ireland but found the daily sectarian tensions dangerous and intolerable. Finally they moved back to Australia for 'a freer life'. Phyllis worked in Dandenong Hospital, applied to McCulloch House and felt she had 'won the lottery' when she was accepted.

'When I came here,' she tells me, 'I didn't have any pallia-tive-care experience. But I had met Jill [unit nurse] at Dandenong, and Dr Ruth Redpath, who were our palliative-care consultants. I liked the way the palliative team looked at the big picture, and I found that if you followed their recom-mendations, you had far better pain control and management. Unlike other medical teams they relished questions and sorting the problems out. I had never seen nursing like that before. It was a totally different way of treating patients and relatives. I knew then it was what I wanted to do.

'Unless you've had physical pain you don't know the depths it can take you to. Pain is like a whirlpool. If you don't catch someone before they're in the middle of it, there can be a tremendous struggle to pull them out. When you get a patient's pain under control, the family's pain is under control. But in ordinary hospitals the whole feeling is different. There's often a sense of fear. Sheets are tied around the bed to hold the patient in. Once you've seen the nursing here, you know there's no need for people to go through what they're going through all the time elsewhere.

'When Graham Davey came back here, he was in trouble. It took us two hours to get his pain under control. We started at the top of the list of opioids and went through them. We gave him the maximum of everything that was ordered, but to no effect. The pain was mostly in his liver area. He couldn't keep his head on the pillow, kept pulling himself down on the bed with his pain. Finally we gave Graham some metazolam, used usually as an anaesthetic. We gave him some, then some more, then a third lot. And he became his normal self.

'We thought he would die that night, but he lived for several days after, was even well enough one day to sit in the sun for a while. He hung on and on. He didn't want to die. He was only forty-six. He didn't feel it was time to die. He was a very bitter man, not only angry but frightened. If a person doesn't believe in life after death, it must be worse. When you see people who are dying, and they have regrets coming at them like ghosts from the past, you realise how good it is to live life without being afraid, and to deal with things as they happen, and not store them away "for the future".

'Many people, especially the Irish, don't like other people to know what's happening. They're fond of secrets. They can't share their lives. Graham couldn't share his. He didn't seem to have any close friends. His associates from his business came once or twice, but he refused to see them. He didn't realise he was denying them something *they* needed. He just didn't seem to trust anybody. All the support had to come from his family.

'People don't always change because they are dying. We've a saying that if you're a bastard when you're living, you'll be the same bastard when you're dying. Their deaths are usually the hardest because they've forgotten how to be human. We try to give them low-key psychological support in small, everyday ways because they're very rejecting of anything more formal.

'Working in palliative care has had a big effect on me. It does on everyone. Occasionally you get a patient who's rude or abusive. Before I came to McCulloch House that would have upset me. I would have wanted to get away from it, or try to stop it. But perhaps because there are no boundaries, no rules here, I have a deep sense of my own worth. I feel in control. All Graham's rudeness did was arouse my compassion, my understanding of how lost he felt, how deeply he was suffering, how he felt it was too early to die but too late to change anything.

'His family stayed with him for the last three days. His wife sat close, but the children farther back, at a distance. You could have cut the tension in the room with a knife. There wasn't any sense of peace. There was grief, though. Perhaps it came from love. I felt it came more from pain and confusion. When you lose someone like your father, and it hasn't been a good relationship, you never have another chance to have a father. Perhaps the wife will later on meet someone and have a happy marriage. But the children, they'll never be able to make up for the way they were deprived. As soon as Graham died, the family left. They looked as if they were escaping.'

Graham Davey, like Michael Fulton, lived a little less than six months after the initial diagnosis of cancer. For three of those months he believed he would make a complete recovery. He accepted chemotherapy treatment, thinking it would cure him. When he realised it was only palliative—an attempt to ease the pain by shrinking the tumour—he felt tricked and cheated.

Graham had actively discouraged his doctors' attempts to communicate with honesty with outbursts of anger. He erected a barrier to truth—based on the irrelevant argument that he had work to do—and continued to hide behind it through all the early stages of his illness. Only when the oncologist asked if he had put his affairs in order did Graham begin to grasp that he would die. Then his response was the response he had made all his adult life to situations that threatened him or thwarted his goals—incredulity, resistance, and anger. Casting himself in the role of someone open to truth—'Why didn't you tell me?'—he then attempted to lay blame on his doctors for his ignorance.

Did brusque and bellicose Graham Davey have another side? Dame Cicely Saunders, who revived the hospice/palliative care movement and has spent her entire adult life with the dying, believes that everyone has a spiritual dimension. By spiritual she doesn't mean a formal religious adherence, but rather 'the whole area of thought concerning moral values throughout life'. Most people, as they approach death, have this spiritual need to find a meaning and purpose to their life.

But Graham Davey was a true psychological casualty of the times. His spiritual aspects were long ago repressed. A deep need to make 'a success' of his life drove him, but what he saw as true and valuable was measured mainly in money and the acquisitions and status that money can buy. Apart from anger and sexual affection, he seemed unable to express genuine emotion. His few friends were business friends, linked together in the common web of money-making. Even so, these friends were willing to offer him a degree of support with phone calls and at least two visits to McCulloch House.

Graham perceived his cancer and accompanying physical weakness as a failure, a type of personal bankruptcy, something foisted on him cruelly and undeservedly. Neither his pride nor his incapacity to trust would allow him to admit his friends to witness what he perceived as 'failure'. His unanswered question was always, 'Why me?'

Sometime early in his life Graham had written a script for himself, a detailed fantasy of the life he would create step by step, and according to his own will. The cancer that he carried could even then have been in his body, for cancer can be carried for years before revealing itself. Graham had never lived with any thought that there could be more to life than met the eye, either physically or spiritually. Being intelligent and middle-aged he was probably not unaware of other dimensions. He simply had no time for them. He had lived his life as if it would go on forever, and he couldn't change when he was dying. His interest in his business affairs remained his prime concern. He had no normal desire to reinforce whatever bonds he had with his family. If he did have a need, he chose, or was unable, to discuss it with anyone.

When Graham died, he left a wife who had waited all her life to be allowed to love him, three fine children, and a multi-million-dollar fortune. Yet he died steeped in psychological pain because the final accomplishment of his life—the building of a shopping mall—was denied him.

How strong were the emotional bonds that linked Joanne to her husband? Bonds don't have to be happy to be strong. Her anger at Graham's failure to give her and the children the emotional support and attention they needed was deeply rooted. Only time will reveal whether she is attached to this anger, or whether she can relinquish it with a sense of relief and liberation.

Her decision to take over Graham's large financial empire is a questionable one. Perhaps it provides a chance to 'prove' herself and her thwarted business abilities to her dead husband. Perhaps she simply feels capable and ready for a major change in her life, or sees the move as a chance to bring the family together in a common enterprise. Or perhaps it is simply her version of payback time.

For years this family was forced to conform to the hopes, desires, and expectations of one dominant figure. In doing so, specific habits and attitudes were formed. For a long time after his death Graham Davey will continue to dominate his family, if only because of the effort they each will need to make to reclaim their true and basic personalities from the effects of his harsh and domineering influence. Perhaps, later on, his children will reconcile themselves to their father's imperfections, be grateful for what he did give them, and forgive him for what he didn't.

# Searching for Meaning

*Between two worlds life hovers like a star,*
*'Twixt night and morn, upon the horizon's verge.*
*How little do we know that which we are!*
*How less what we may be!*
  —Lord Byron, *Don Juan*

I've been provided with a small office in a strategic spot. Fortunately—because I've needed some help in settling in—the offices of the McCulloch House director Michael Ashby and his administrative assistant, Janis Keogh, are above at the top of the broad staircase. That of head unit nurse Jill Fletcher is a couple of doors down. As the days pass, though, I find I'm spending most of my time in the lounge. There I can keep tabs on everything that is going on. I can see the main desk, hear the chatter, observe nurses coming and going and watch visitors walking up the steep curve to the main door. When a new patient arrives, usually by ambulance or wheelchair, Wendy, the ward clerk, hurries outside, rain or shine, to welcome him or her and introduce any staff members who are around.

The surprised response of most patients to the warm

greetings and interest created by their arrival is revealing. Obviously the sounds and sights of normal life are the last thing they expect—not a uniform in sight, everyone dressed as if in their own home, music from the radio in the lounge, the resident cat curled up on one of the chairs, a visitor making a cup of tea, a couple of patients sitting outside smoking, a family dog asleep on a patient's bed. Close to death, these new patients are being placed in the middle of life. Preserving an atmosphere of normality is part of palliative care, and relates directly to the nurturing of a sense of peace, continuity, and meaning.

When we come to die, we often seek a meaning for our lives. What was it all about? Where did all the years go? Did they have any meaning? Did I do what I could have done with them? What was the purpose of it all? Did I fulfil it? Was I just a glitch in time and space? When a patient has the time and serenity to prepare for his or her own death, those who work in palliative care often see these questions arise.

I try to imagine how I will respond when my life enters its final stage. Will all my interest in work, politics, art, and theatre dissipate? If so, what will be left of me? Remove all those interests and dreams that have fleshed out my life and what will the bones of my being look like? What will count?

Harry Symonds is about to tell me what counts, at least with him. On several occasions I have noticed him emerge from his room and wander around for some light-hearted repartee with the nurses. A slightly stooped grey-haired man in a midnight-blue dressing-gown, he seems to thrive on being sociable. He always holds a cloth to the side of his face and, on inquiring, I am told he has a sarcoma of the mouth that extends into his jaw and neck.

On this particular day we run into each other at the desk.

He introduces himself, says he would be delighted to talk with me, and ushers me back to his room. The left side of Harry's face is greatly swollen, his lower lip is misshapen, and he constantly has to sop up the spittle that drips from a mouth he can no longer close.

Until I went to McCulloch House I thought of cancer as contained within the body and had only a limited idea how malevolent it can be when it breaks through to the surface. It is as if Harry has two faces. Above the damage wrought by cancer is a good head of hair, a fine-shaped, slightly mottled nose, a pair of blue eyes that sparkle with mischief and humour, and a network of laughter wrinkles that trace a cobweb of white lines in a weathered face. He tells me to take a seat, and I slide into an armchair while he gets onto the bed, saying in a gentlemanly fashion that he hopes I don't mind but he is feeling a bit tuckered.

After I tell him what I want, he laughs and says, 'My life story? Nobody's ever asked me for that before. Makes me feel…I dunno. What are you going to do with it? Make it into a movie?'

'Yes, with Arnie Schwarzenegger in the lead role,' I say.

That idea makes us both laugh. There is an impishness in this sixty-four-year-old that encourages a bit of sauciness. I go on to explain what I am doing, and he wants to know if I am interested in him 'because of this', tapping the side of his face. I say partly. What really interests me is in finding out how, when he is so sick, he is still so happy. I refrain from saying right then that because of his type of cancer I am interested in his views on euthanasia. I also want to know who else in his family has had cancer and if this has influenced his views.

'Happy?' he says. 'I'm happy all right. I've been so lucky, you wouldn't believe it.' He turns to me full face and beams, covering the bottom half of his face with a towel. 'I've had a great life! Didn't become the governor-general…' At this his eyes dance. Here is a man at ease with himself. 'Never wanted to be one of the rich and famous, ha, ha. Got a few regrets, mind you.'

I suggest he tells me about his life and what counted.

'I can tell you right off what counts, Lisa.' He is totally intent in what he wants to say, and I am delighted that he can so easily slip into using my first name. 'Friends, friends and family. That's it. If you've got friends and family, you've got everything. Mind you, I wouldn't mind getting rid of this.' He touches the side of his face. 'But that's up to the old fella upstairs.' He gestures with a flip of his hand skyward.

'Well, here goes. I was born in Melbourne at the Queen Victoria Hospital. It's gone now. We lived in North Melbourne. There were five kids. Both my parents were Aussies. My father's dad was Irish, but my mother's was Presbyterian.'

Chuckling at his own little family joke, Harry is distracted by a plethora of spit that needs immediate attention. After he delicately wipes it up, he continues. 'Dad's name was Frank, my mother's was Grace. Dad was a sparrow starver, we used to call them, you know, a garbage collector. Every morning at six Dad would walk two miles to work to the Melbourne City Depot. He'd get home after 5 p.m. and he'd often bring something he'd found in the garbage, like an old fruit case or some kindling. If it was too heavy, he'd take a tram, but he didn't like doing that. Dad earned two pounds ten a week, and it was a struggle.

'Mum did everything: washing in the big copper boiler, ironing, darning. A hole in a sock, out came the wool and cotton. Nothing got thrown out. All the clothes were hand-me-downs.' Harry shakes his head slowly and breathes deeply, as if remembrance of his mother's life fills him with a tender awe.

'I went to Errol Street State School, where they'd give you a whack with a ruler if you got out of line. Not that I ever did, mind you, ha, ha. At ten I started selling newspapers, the *Herald* and the *Sporting Globe*, at the corner of Flemington Road and Abbotsford Street, North Melbourne. Remember the *Globe*, a big pink paper? People'd almost knock me down to get one, it was that popular. I had that spot for four years, jumping on and off the moving trams, hanging on the side, handing over papers, making change, yelling "He-raald!" If I got two and six a week, I'd keep sixpence and give the rest to Mum. A milkshake only cost tuppence ha'penny.

'Our house had seven bedrooms, a big old brick place. Our uncle and aunt lived with us, too. The loo was at least thirty yards down the backyard. There was a loft down there, too, with a stable for horses. Every Saturday night Mum would heat up some buckets of water and we'd have a bath, whether we needed it or not.'

His shoulder shakes with silent laughter, and he looks at me with his head to the side with a shy, playful grin. 'The five of us would use the same water.'

'The kids today don't know half of it. Of course, in some ways they weren't on our backs all the time like they are with kids today. In other ways it was worse. Once Brian—he's my brother—and I just missed the bus going to the footy, so we hung on to the spare tyre at the back and went that way. You know, nobody said anything to us—all the way through town with cars just behind us and we could've fallen off! We'd pick up bottles at the footy, and with twenty-four you'd get a shilling. We could go to the pictures on Saturday with that and buy a box of Jaffas.'

He rests for a moment and then remarks, as if choosing from a series of treasured old scenes rolling by in his head, 'Christmas was the best time of the year. All year long Dad saved the bottles and rags he found in the garbage. He'd carry them, walking all the way home from work, and keep them in the old stable, and at the end of the year he'd sell the lot. We'd get ten pounds out of it, and that was our Christmas. We all got presents and we always had a turkey.'

Harry's last words contain a hundred years of family history. He pauses in the presence of his precious memories. It strikes me how unlikely it is that his dad, walking three kilometres home carrying kindling, or his mum, bent over a wood stove while the temperature hit the century mark, would have imagined the strength their son would derive from these images of love sixty years later.

'We had an uncle in the bush, working in Dimboola, and he'd send a live turkey in a cage. Dad would chop its head off— we weren't too keen on seeing that—and there was someone down the road who'd pluck it for us. Mum would cook it in a cast-iron pot in the wood stove. It'd be about 100 degrees some Christmas days, but we had the wood stove going flat out. We'd have uncles and aunts, about twenty people in for dinner. Every year the same thing happened. Then after dinner Mum and Dad would give us threepence each, and we'd go to the baths next to the North Melbourne football ground. I guess they wanted to be rid of us for a bit.

'At fifteen I started as an apprentice at a bookbinder as a guillotine operator. It's my only regret, well, that and what happened to my marriage. My parents thought of it. In those days to get a job was very important. If you weren't a student, you had to have an apprenticeship. I did a six-year apprenticeship at seven and six a week. I stuck it out.' He turns his head away as he covers the entire lower half of his face with a cloth, taking his time cleaning up. Finally he says, 'I didn't like bookbinding, but I stuck with it for six years. Slave labour, you'd say these days.'

Once Harry completed his apprenticeship, he left bookbinding, worked on roads for a while 'in the stinking heat', and then got a job as a salesman with Leo Hemingway & Pickett, a tobacco distributor, later taken over by W. D. & H. O. Wills. Along the way he got married. Five children were born, but the marriage 'went on the skids and finally broke up'.

'I'm separated from my wife, Mary, but not divorced. That isn't easy.' He pauses, looking out the window at nothing, thoughtfully pressing the cloth against his face. 'I've had my ups and downs.' There is another long silence, then he says, 'Yeah, but I've really enjoyed my life, going to the RSL, playing the pokies, having my four or five stubbies—always VB—a day.' Harry hesitates, looks slightly abashed, then offers, 'Yeah, and I also smoked about forty cigarettes a day. Won't be having another.' He falls quiet again, then says defiantly, 'But I'm not changing anything else!'

'How did the cancer start?' I ask.

'Well, I've got false teeth. Just a year ago I thought I had an ulcer under the bottom plate. That went on for about two and a half months, but it was worse than an ulcer, so I went to the GP and he said I'd have to see a surgeon. It was four weeks before I could get in, then they did a biopsy. I went back a week later, and the doc said it was cancer. I had a lot of X-rays, and they said I'd have to go to Monash Medical Centre to see which way they'd attack it.

'I really don't remember what details they gave me. Not much I could do about it. I saw the surgeon towards the end of September, and two weeks later they took my lower jaw out, took bone out of my left leg, and made a new jaw with it. It wasn't a success. And I got a terrible staph infection in my leg, but no point in going on about that. Anyway, then they did a second op to pin the jaw in and hold it up, and a third to put a screw into the jaw. It was wired for five weeks and I couldn't talk. I came good, though, and a fortnight later went to my brother and sister-in-law's home in Brighton.'

As Harry is speaking, his brother and sister-in-law, Brian and Anne arrive. Affectionate greetings are exchanged all around, introductions are made, and there is laughter. Brian is a hero in football circles, a former captain of the North Melbourne Football Club and for some years chairman of selectors. They are a strikingly attractive couple, and their love for Harry fills the room like a huge bouquet of flowers.

'I was pretty down, wasn't I, Brian, when I went to your place?' It was clear his younger brother was his hero. Harry told me he has barracked for North Melbourne for fifty years, but that he only got to play for Camberwell in Association football, which was 'second-best' in those days.

'Not "your" place, Harry,' Anne interjects. 'It's *your* place, *your* home. Yes, you were pretty down.'

Harry turns to me with a look that says, 'Isn't she something? See what I mean about what really counts in life?'

Then he continues. 'Honest to god, Lisa, I didn't know whether to shoot myself or hang myself. I was so low. I felt I couldn't ever get up again. If someone had offered me a shot of something to finish it all off, I'd have taken it. My family kept me hanging on—Brian and Anne, my brother, my sister and my youngest son. Ah, they were so good to me.' Harry unabashedly wipes his eyes. 'I tell you, a lot of prayers were said, and finally I came good.'

'One day Brian and I were talking about old times. I had

such good memories of home, and suddenly I wanted to go back to North Melbourne, look around, and walk up the back lanes. "Why don't we do it?" I said, just like that, spontaneously. I'd never really thought of doing that before. And we did. Spent an afternoon wandering around all the old haunts. Brought back a lot of memories.' Harry's eyes sparkle, as if he can see himself and Brian still hanging onto the back of a bus.

Palliative-care nurses visited Harry every day in Brighton to change the dressing and ensure he had no pain. However, the side of his face continued to swell and then his neck started to puff out. As soon as he mentioned having 'a fair bit' of pain, his palliative-care nurses arranged for him to enter McCulloch House to adjust his medication.

'I'd heard about McCulloch House but never dreamed it'd be such a happy-go-lucky place,' Harry insists. 'You hear you're going to a palliative care place and you're between Arthur and Martha. You've got to stop the pain, but your heart drops. You think: this is it. You don't know what's coming down and you've got no control. In a regular hospital you can feel that, nobody's fault, the nurses all have their hands full. But when I got here, well, I think I'd imagined something quiet, deadly, a bit of a morgue. But as soon as I came through the front door, Wendy was there with that sunny smile of hers, and then Jill, and I felt more like my old self. Not coming totally good again, but a bit more of life. I've always enjoyed my life. Even when things were down, I knew they'd come up again.

'When you're sick, I tell you, you can hear whether people mean what they say, or whether they're just trying to be nice. It's clear as night from day. You couldn't fake what goes on around here, the way everyone enjoys a good laugh. You know, I totally forget about this.' He taps his face. 'I feel I'm still good for a bit of life yet. Michael [Ashby] and Peter [Martin] have got the pain under control, and I'm going home in a couple of days. I plan to go out, go to the RSL, play the pokies, have my beer, play a bit of golf.'

'He has a terrific attitude,' Brian tells me. 'He never sits in the chair and says, "Bugger this, I've had enough."'

Brian's words seem to contradict Harry's statement that he didn't know 'whether to hang himself or shoot himself'. Is Brian trying to foster hope? It gives me an opening to get their views on euthanasia.

'I agree with it,' Harry says without a second's hesitation. 'I know you're not supposed to do yourself in, but I'm not worried about the old fella upstairs. He'd understand. He's used to us.' Harry speaks as if he has just hung up the phone after talking with Him.

'Our sister had a tumour of the bone,' Brian says. 'The last three months she was a vegetable. You didn't want to go and see her it upset you so much. It's a nonexistent life. Anne and I, we've told each other we don't want to go on if we're like that.'

I ask about another end-of-life matter—the termination of life-support treatments that would then allow death to occur naturally. This is an option, say, in the case of an accident. Have they made out any sort of Living Will, or designated any relative or friend as having medical power of attorney to ensure someone could make the decisions they want if they themselves are incapable of doing so?

'No,' Anne replies. 'We know what we'd want, and we've told each other. We've never put it in writing, though. I'd just never thought of that, both of us being hurt at the same time.'

As I leave, Harry says, 'Listen, Lisa, I want a copy of this book. When's it coming out?'

'Maybe June 1998,' I say.

He laughs. 'Oh, shit! You know where I'll be by then.'

Harry went home with Brian and Anne two days later and enjoyed life for six weeks until he had a haemorrhage. He then entered Caritas Christi, another long-established Melbourne hospice. Although he had the option of returning home, Harry decided to stay at Caritas Christi because he feared having another bleed.

Marjorie is a fifty-five-year-old senior physiotherapist and age-care specialist at Monash Medical Centre. Tall and fair-haired, she exudes a quiet competence and strength and works under a tight hospital budget that allows her a scant forty-five minutes per day for McCulloch House patients. She prefers listening to talking and I tell her I am puzzled as to what a physiotherapist can give to a terminally ill patient. Marjorie replies that her palliative-care work gives her 'the greatest satisfaction' of all her work, then explains why.

'Our body image allows us to present ourselves to the world, and when that body image is diminished, there's a feeling that cancer is infiltrating every part of us, robbing us of our integrity. People say, "I just want to be able to walk a little" or "I'd just like to look like my old self". When the body doesn't function as well as it did, a person can feel a huge sense of failure and become extremely depressed.

'We all have a body image. Whether people are satisfied or dissatisfied with it, when they lose it they feel attacked. Body image is your capacity to be yourself, and when you lose it you're compromised. So what I do is set functional goals for that person that allows them to preserve their self-esteem. Self-esteem is very tied in to body image. So I look for goals that allow a person to achieve dignity, pleasure, comfort. They may be small, small things. With someone like Harry, it would be encouraging them not to eat their meals in bed but to sit in an armchair, or to go to the toilet by themselves. These are small things, but big for the person because of their diminished level. It helps retain their body image and supports their sense of worth.

'Massage is very important. All the staff here have been taught to do simple massage, rubbing the hands, feet, legs. You can still feel the sensual side of massage when you're ill, and patients really enjoy it. The message isn't only comfort. It says, "Because you have cancer that doesn't mean I don't want to touch you."'

Touch is the one thing the aged are really deprived of, Marjorie says. Having someone brush their hair or hold and stroke their hand, rub their neck or back, all those reassuring things are completely missing from their lives. Massage reminds people of a normal life, and for this reason she is very keen on it.

'Deep breathing is also very important,' she informs me. 'It's relaxing and helps clear infections. And when breathing becomes compromised, knowing how to do it properly gives you something to focus on, something calming that also helps you remain very aware.

'None of what I do is wasted. I feel that strongly. Giving them some heat, a little movement, some simple exercises. Yes, they're going to die, but that doesn't matter. They still love accomplishing something. They'll say to me, "Look, Marjorie, look how far I can stretch my legs!" And there's a sense of achievement and self-esteem. We're not talking about disease control in palliative care, or prolonging life. Just that life matters, and so it matters how we live it right to the end.'

Marjorie says she has no religion. Her mother was religious, and her father did everything to counteract that religion.

Marjorie left the church when she went to university. But she feels it never entirely left, that something remained, even though the practicalities didn't mean anything to her.

'There's a thing of beauty people have inside them, and you can recognise it in a patient or a staff member. I don't know what to call it. It's not religion or faith in the old sense. It has everything to do with the recognition of a person as a person, as you find them now, not with what will happen, or has happened to them, but as they are in that moment.

'I'm not saying everyone who works here has it—this knowledge, care, and wisdom—but those who haven't got it want it, and are moving towards it. When cancer has destroyed a lot of what we normally think of as beautiful or important in a person, we're open to their essence.'

Marjorie has found working in palliative care to be a humbling experience, not only because of the patients but because of the staff. The ambience is different. How to describe it? A 'tangible spirituality' perhaps. Whatever it is, she believes she has gained a deeper spiritual maturity from dealing daily with the fact of death.

When Harry Symonds first spoke with me, I believed we were simply socialising, a pleasant chat devoid of any significance. From the advantage of years, Harry observed his own boyish antics and those of his brothers and friends, and drew immense pleasure from these memories. He enjoyed his own jokes, which often were aimed at himself, and relished swapping jokes with me. Although assaulted by cancer, which beat up his face, neck, and head into a swollen mass, much as a robber-assailant would, he seemed to stand outside of this finale of his life. When this thought struck me, I realised that Harry was finding in the reiteration of the memories of his youth not only vitality and strength, but a sense of meaning in his life.

Harry has had an ordinary life, a life whose features are instantly recognisable to anyone growing up at any time, anywhere, in pre-1950s Australia. He was raised by two hardworking thrifty parents in an atmosphere of affection, strong family loyalty, observance of traditions, self-reliance and integrity.

He spoke simply and directly. He thought as deeply as most people but, like many of us, wasn't given to complicated speculative or philosophic meanderings. Clearly his great legacy from his parents was that they didn't alienate him from his interior self. When he was a child, they had let him be who he was. They made the error of apprenticing him at fifteen to a trade he had no soul for, but it was a mistake made through ignorance and concern that he have 'a future'. Although there was a slight bitterness in Harry about this, it wasn't directed at his parents.

It occurred to me that Harry had twice said with a tinge of pride that he had 'stuck it out', as if the experience of sticking it out had, in the long run, given him something, not a job but something else. What could that be? Then, looking at him as he bent to clean his face, I thought perhaps it was the ability to endure with patience. Christians call it 'the gift of fortitude' and regard it as one of the cardinal virtues. Buddhists call it 'patient endurance' and hold it to be the most fundamental and most fruitful of all spiritual practices.

Harry allowed himself to weep briefly in front of me—referred to the fact that there had been 'lots of praying'—and did so with confidence, an empathy for his own situation, and even a sense of modest authority of having every right to do so. When assessing his life, Harry described himself as 'so lucky you wouldn't believe it'. There was no, 'Why is this happening to me?' or 'What have I done to deserve this?' Nothing but an acknowledgment of great satisfaction and joy. When I asked Harry what really counted in life, the answer sprang out in an explosion of feeling: 'Family and friends, that's it.'

Because Harry was in McCulloch House for a respite period, our time together was limited. From what time we did have he clearly searched for meaning in the relationship of his life to the real world, to actual events outside of himself, rather than in any mulling around in his own psyche. It is possible that in these memories he found a common thread that, running through the years, wove itself into a meaning. Whatever meaning he might have found was deeply personal, not one shared in our brief acquaintance, and perhaps never specifically articulated to anyone. I believe it was contained within his ability to re-create and revitalise, in the present, the love he had experienced as a child, and with the utmost confidence to run the thread of that love into his brief future and up to 'the fella upstairs'.

I found Harry's ease in relating to a deity significant because of his professed belief in euthanasia. This belief was based in part on his sister's ordeal with cancer. He was untroubled by any ethical considerations. What he had seen his sister endure convinced him of its moral allowability. He was very specific in his belief that 'the fella upstairs' comprehended all human acts. Yet although Harry theoretically believed in euthanasia, in practice he believed more in life. Otherwise he would have killed himself.

Harry's unarticulated search for meaning is a phenomenon shared by many approaching death. In the normal sense, Harry had nothing to live for, yet he felt that by going on living with his cancer he was giving meaning, not only to his life, but to life.

He had *chosen his attitude*, not in a deliberate, conscious manner, but *by acting out who he really was*—a man of courage and hope. Like Michael Fulton, he hadn't given in to despair. He had maintained hope, not for a cure, but for a few more good days playing golf and having a couple of beers and a meeting with a compassionate and understanding 'fella upstairs'.

One final factor emerged from talking with this genial man. Those working with the terminally ill have noted that the desire to fulfil a long-procrastinated pleasure is a recurring phenomenon with the terminally ill. Maurice Abiven, honorary president of France's Palliative Care Society, has cited the desire people have to hear a particular piece of music, have a special meal, or see one particular person. In Harry's case it was revisiting the area where he had spent his childhood and wandering through it at leisure with members of his family. Abiven wrote of this phenomenon in the hope that family members and carers would become aware that a patient's wish, puzzling and even bizarre to others, deserves respect. It expresses something with which the patient identifies, has long wanted but put off, but now needs for a sense of self-fulfilment.

The brief discussion with Harry's family, Anne and Brian, regarding end-of-life decisions was informative. Neither wished to be put on life-support systems or to endure treatment procedures that would prolong their lives if they were left in a totally incompetent physical or mental state. The law in Victoria allows for anyone over the age of sixteen to appoint, in advance, a medical agent to act for them in the event of an accident or illness, and to consent or refuse any treatment on their behalf. This would normally involve being taken off a ventilator or the cessation of all drugs, interventions and food so that the natural process of death could occur.

The intervention of medical technology at the end of our

lives, and the extension of an unwanted, no-quality life, is one of our greatest nightmares, yet few of us have done anything to preclude it. Empowering someone you trust to look after your health-care decisions should you become incapable of doing so isn't difficult. Margaret Brown, a health-care professional whose study of the legal and social contingencies of introducing a medical power of attorney in South Australia formed the basis of her master's thesis, sees the issue as one of patient empowerment, and a move away from the paternalistic notion of 'doctors know best'.

I identified with Anne and Brian. At least they had discussed the issue and, if push came to shove, this verbal discussion, even without legal papers, would carry some authority. I hadn't made out a Living Will (although I have done so since), nor had I even discussed it with anybody, because, for heaven's sake, *everyone would know* I wouldn't want to be hooked up to a machine.

What this aversion reflects is simply our inability to comprehend we are going to die. Sigmund Freud pointed this out—that our consciousness cannot grasp its own end. We *know* that our enemies will die, and are willing to concede that even our friends will. But we believe we won't.

# Pain

*Be near me when the sensuous frame*
*Is racked with pains that conquer trust;*
*And Time, a maniac scattering dust,*
*And Life, a Fury slinging flame.*
  —Lord Alfred Tennyson, 'In Memoriam A. H. H.'

A fair percentage of dying patients in acute-care hospitals are suffering some degree of pain. Many of the doctors, nurses and visiting specialists were educated in the 1960s and 1970s when there was widespread fear of opioids causing addiction, tolerance and respiratory depression. Even today this outmoded idea, combined with staff shortages, tight budgets and increased pressure can result in human cruelty.

At McCulloch House pain is treated like the enemy. The staff treat every patient professionally in a highly individualised manner. They are aware that there is no set 'right' dose, no set 'right' combinations of opioids, drugs and other medications. Different individuals require different amounts and combinations of drugs to bring their pain under control. Because doctors and nurses don't regard the patient as an object under control, they listen respectfully to what the patient has to say and act on it. They tend to their patients as if to acknowledge that 'there but for the grace of God go I'.

Pain control at McCulloch House reflects the beliefs of the director, Professor Michael Ashby, an oncologist by training and an internationally respected authority on pain management. He regards under-treatment of cancer pain as a significant problem in the practice of medicine. In an article entitled 'Hard Cases, Causation, and Care of the Dying' in the *Journal of Law and Medicine*, Professor Ashby states his position. 'It is a common belief, and the basis of a considerable body of legal and legislative opinion, that morphine dose is the main determinant of whether the drug causes or hastens death. In fact, there is no such determinative or threshold dose, and this approach is flawed. What matters is the present dose in relation to the previous dose. It is [therefore] the size of the initial dose and the rate of subsequent increases which are important.'*

Further on in the same article he writes, 'Despite an extensive and sustained international campaign (by the World Health Organisation) many doctors still believe that they are causing or hastening the death of patients by this process [of adjusting the regular dose upward], despite the absence of any evidence to support this view.'

In other words, Professor Ashby doesn't believe there is any established maximum 'safe' dose of morphine and teaches that it should be increased until a patient's pain is controlled. Morphine dose escalation is not subject to upper limits at McCulloch House, whereas non-opioid drugs are. According to Professor Ashby, many patients get relief with dosages that could be considered quite moderate. When this relief is needed,

* Michael Ashby, 'Hard Cases, Causation, and Care of the Dying', *Journal of Law and Medicine.*

it is given. No clock controls or times it. What respect for the rights and individuality of the patient is there when a patient is told: 'You'll have to wait'?

However, when a patient arrives at McCulloch House and his or her first words are 'I want to die', which happens from time to time, the staff does not oblige. There are two reasons for this. One is that it often happens that when a patient's pain is relieved he or she doesn't want to die. Joy at having a few more days in which to savour life replaces the desire for death. The other reason is that the duty of a palliative-care centre is to use every means possible to obviate pain, not to kill patients.

One occasion I am on the spot when a woman arrives stating loudly that she wants to end it all. Visiting her the next day, my stomach in knots over what I may find, I am astounded to have her tell me that, regardless of what she said, death isn't what she wants. She simply wanted to end her pain. Once that was gone, so was any wish for death. Suddenly, like Michael Fulton and Harry Symonds, she remembered many small reasons to live, words to be spoken, tasks to be completed.

Experienced palliative-care doctors can bring the most aggressive pain under control in most cases. But in an estimated 5 per cent of patients (this figure varies slightly depending on the study) they can't. Having seen the intensity of pain that a cancer patient can suffer, my initial reaction was to think this five per cent should constitute the franchise allowed to vote on the euthanasia issue. All others would be excluded on the basis that their arguments, either way, were merely mental constructs, founded on theoretical or speculative grounds and as such not necessarily related to any reality. However, when I recall Dame Cicely Saunders' words, 'None of us are going to get out of this alive', I realise that the type of death facing us is such a lottery that we all have the right to vote on euthanasia.

This 95 per cent total pain-free success rate is acceptable to our society. Could that be because the dead can't speak? Or is it more a case of the good of the whole society needing to take precedence over the good of a small number of individuals in that society? Are 5 per cent of sufferers sufficient to validate the legalisation of euthanasia? The only recourse for relief available to this 5 per cent is to be sedated into a state of total unconsciousness that is maintained until death arrives. This practice is medically and legally acceptable. It is pragmatic and it is as humane as the law currently allows. Is it good enough? What would we hear if those 5 per cent of sufferers could speak? Would they say, 'In my acceptance of suffering, which couldn't be avoided, I found the real meaning of my life'? Or would they say, 'Curse you for having had the means to end my suffering and refusing to do so'?

After several weeks at McCulloch House, I speak to Paul Dilorenzo and his daughter-in-law, Nina, about their experiences in the terminal illness of Paul's wife, Eva, who died at McCulloch House on 22 November 1996. This is one case where no doubt exists that, if euthanasia were permitted, the family of Eva would have chosen it for her.

'Eva was born in Alexandria, Egypt,' Paul says. He is a slight, wiry man whose manners and dress give the impression of reticence and decency. 'I was born there, too. My grandparents emigrated to Egypt from Italy. Egypt was our home, Italy our roots. Eva's parents were Cypriot Greeks. Her real name was Eleanor, but she preferred Eva.

'I met her one afternoon when I went to the cinema. She

was working there as an usherette. In a uniform, little hat'—
Paul's hands gesture at the side of his head as if to straighten a
bellboy's matchbox hat—'she really took my eye. Her father
was very cautious about me, even visited my boss to investigate
me, make sure I was suitable for his daughter. That was 1952
and the war [in Cyprus] was going on. He finally approved,
and Eva and I were married. We left Egypt straightaway for
Australia and we never regretted it.

'Eva's older brother had already gone to Melbourne, and so
had an aunt. Eva was twenty-two and I was twenty-eight. We
moved into the aunt's garage. After a bit I got a job as an
electrical welder, and when we got a small down payment
together we bought a house in Clayton. It cost £3850 pounds
and our payment was fifteen pounds a month. I was earning
sixty a month, so it was exactly one-fourth of my salary.' As he
recalls these details, which reveal so much care, so much penny-
pinching, so many dreams of strangers in a wonderful,
bewildering land, he smiles with a mix of pride and humility.
Eva, he says, loved to look smart, loved for things to be just
right.

'When Eva and I left Egypt, my mother and brother went to
live in Italy. But three years after we got here, my brother
arrived, and four years after that my mother came. Eva and I
had two sons, Matthew and Mario. So we had a big family
here. I stayed with the same company, General Motors, for
thirty years. Twelve years ago we sold our old home and bought
one at Middle Brighton.

'Eva used to get ulcers from time to time. We'd been up at
Surfers Paradise, this was in November 1995, and when we
returned she thought her ulcers were back. She didn't get any
better and went to see her doctor. She was looking jaundiced.
She'd had a kidney stone removed four years earlier, and the

doctor thought there was another blocking the bile duct.'

The doctor said he was about to go on holidays, told them to go back home, and he would call when he returned in two weeks. At this point in the story Paul pauses. His daughter-in-law Nina puts her hand on his arm and takes up the account for him.

'Mum [Eva] had a lot of pain in those two weeks and went into hospital. I was there when she asked the nurse if they'd gotten the stone out, and the nurse said, "I'll call the other nurse." And when the other nurse came in she said, "I'll call the doctor." When the specialist came, he said the X-rays showed spots on Eva's chest. His words were: "The horse has already bolted." We were shocked. It was the day of the massacre in Tassie [on 28 April 1996, a twenty-nine-year-old named Martin Bryant killed thirty-five tourists with a semi-automatic rifle at Port Arthur in southern Tasmania], and Eva asked him, "What can I do?" His reply was: "This isn't a tragedy. The massacre is the tragedy."

'We felt sick and lost. We didn't know what to do, except we had to get out, get away from there. Mum came home and we had the twenty-four-hour visiting nurse service from Dandenong. Over four months Mum had four doses of chemotherapy. Out of six months she had a total of one good month. During this time, she and Paul had their fortieth wedding anniversary. We had a white stretch limo pick them up, and then all of us went to the top of the Regent Hotel. The fortieth is the ruby anniversary, so we gave them a wedding picture with a ruby in the centre of the frame. Eva had been feeling very poor, but that night for some reason she felt good. She dressed exquisitely for the occasion. I'll never forget how beautiful she looked.'

Nina says they all believed the chemotherapy had 'done the

trick', that the tumour had ceased growing. But then Eva started having back pain. She couldn't get comfortable. She thought it was a sciatic nerve. In early October her son Matthew rang the doctor and said, 'Mum can hardly walk.' The doctor put the family in touch with Dr Peter Martin. Eva was mystified and wanted to know why on earth she should go to a palliative-care centre since that was where people went to die. Finally the doctor decided to tell her: 'Eva,' she said, 'you've got six months to live.'

'Mum blanked out everything the doctors and nurses said to her,' Nina tells me. 'And then she'd say to us, "What did they say?" Throughout the whole thing she didn't believe she was dying. We had to be very careful what we said to her regarding the truth. She'd ask for us to tell her what was happening and then didn't want to hear it.'

Eva had the option of going home, but she didn't want to die there. More than anything she dreaded going home and then having to leave. She found that pain almost as unbearable as her physical pain, which by then filled her entire torso, an ache dull and deep with explosions of short, sharp stabbing pain. So she stayed at McCulloch House.

'You were never left alone here,' Nina says. 'If you were sitting by her bed, someone would always come in and keep you company. Mum still had hope until the very week before she passed away. But then she said she wanted to die, she'd had enough. She was getting 3200 milligrams of morphine a day, but she was in a lot of pain.

'Five days before the end, her grand-daughter came to see her. Mum said to me, "Nina, go and buy me a nice new nightie." She was always so chic. She wanted everything to look nice and new. She'd dyed her hair for years, but now it was showing some grey and she couldn't stand that. She was in agony, but with the help of Irene [a trained enrolled nurse] we managed to dye her hair in bed.

'She died at a quarter to eight in the evening. Irene told us to keep talking to her, that she could hear all we were saying. But then an unexpected thing happened. A priest walked into her room. It shocked us. I felt really upset and asked, maybe angrily, "Why have you come?" He said, "I was just driving by and Eva's face appeared to me and I thought I'd pop in to see her. I felt she was calling me." He then blessed her, putting his hand on the side of her head. When he did that, Eva let out a huge sigh of relief, as if to say, "I can go now." We then combed her hair and sprayed a little perfume on her. Eva opened her eyes for a moment, then died.

'When Matthew and Mario arrived a few minutes later, Irene met them at the door, opened her arms and hugged them. That's what this place is like. I could bring my children here, and the volunteers played with them. We were told everything we wanted to know. My husband sat down with Peter [Martin], and the talk left him feeling so much better.

'I can't tell you the difference being able to talk to the doctor makes. We were so devastated with that first specialist coming at us. All we'd said was, "What can we do?" When we came here, if there were five doctors lined up down the hall waiting to get a word with Michael [Ashby], he'd still talk to you as if he had all the time in the world. Even though months have passed, when I go to McCulloch House people remember who I am.

'The whole experience has brought us together.' Nina shakes her head emphatically. 'But Eva suffered too much. Sitting on the toilet, crying, hating to see herself that way. She lost her dignity. I really believe in euthanasia. I don't know how we'd be feeling right now if she had been given a shot and put out of it.

But I never want to go through what she did.'

'I'm a Catholic,' Paul says, 'but they put an animal to sleep that suffers like that. She was my wife, but a dog would have been let go. I believe in euthanasia. If I want to die, and I'm near the end, why let me suffer? I'm not afraid of death any more, but I am afraid of cancer. She suffered too much.'

I am eating lunch in a staff room where the lavishness of window size and ceiling height reflect the confidence and grandeur of this country a hundred years ago. I am talking to Robert, a quiet, thoughtful nurse in his late thirties. The youngest of five children, Robert was raised on a farm near Byron Bay, New South Wales. He completed a three-year university land-surveying course, didn't like it, did various jobs, volunteered at a centre for the disabled and discovered he liked caring for others. While skiing at Mount Buller in Victoria, he met a group of nurses who loved their work. He then entered Royal Melbourne to train as a nurse, shocking his usually supportive family who couldn't believe he would 'throw away his degree'. Soon after, he married Maria, one of the nurses he had met at Buller. She works in the mother and baby unit of a Melbourne hospital, and together they raise their three children.

'I look forward to coming to work,' Robert tells me, 'more so than any job I've ever had. Just to be a part of people's lives at this point is deeply satisfying. Sometimes people confronting their own deaths are terrified and we can do a lot for them. We stay with them, talk to them, bring their pain under control, get rid of their nausea and agitation, and when they die they're quite peaceful. It's the same with the families. They're so confused by death. They've never been near it before. They're terribly anxious and agitated. And then this environment gets to them and they open up and relax.

'Some patients don't have anyone, a migrant perhaps who's led an insular life, or for some reason is cut off. They lean on you, take you into their confidence. You feel so privileged to be part of it, to be able to help.

'My perception of Mrs Dilorenzo's pain, well, we sedated her, but to an extent that was against the grain. The family wanted her very sedated. She did have extreme pain at first. The family asked for euthanasia. Families say, "You wouldn't treat a dog like that. Haven't you got an injection?" Others say, "I don't know how you can work in this environment without doing something." Usually this sentiment comes from the family. The patient is much too sick usually, but occasionally they ask for it. Often, though, it's the family pushing for euthanasia. I'm very conscious that we can walk in and out, we can go home, and switch off a little. I'm always aware of that.

'What happened in the Northern Territory, well, there's always someone whose suffering isn't relieved by medication and they want death. Always.' On 25 May 1995, the Northern Territory Assembly passed, by a single vote, the Rights of the Terminally Ill Act, which legalised doctor-assisted suicide. The law went into effect on 1 July 1996. Some eight months later, in March 1997, the federal government overrode the act on the grounds that the powers of the territorial assembly weren't those of a state assembly and lacked the authority to pass any law legalising any form of euthanasia.

'Despite the big debate whether euthanasia is on or not,' Robert continues, 'I've worked in oncology-symptom management and it's not good. Hospitals can't get off their acute-care mentality. It would make all the difference if they could. People are dying in atrocious circumstances. I don't think euthanasia needs to be legislated and medically sanctioned and all the Ts crossed and in place. It doesn't need the involvement of doctors and parliament to sanction it. I just wish it was left with the family and patient, and that patients would make their wishes clear, or that there'd be some designated family person.

'Palliative-care nursing is a different kind of nursing. You have to be very flexible and you have to enjoy spending a lot of time with the patient. We have the luxury here to do that. All nurses can do the physical things for the patient and the family, but then the work is only half done. But some nurses don't want the emotional side of nursing. A nurse's view can be very warped. To nurse well emotional balance is needed, not a skewed reality. If your style of work is task-oriented—do this, do that—it wouldn't work here.

'In twenty years the baby boomers will be dying and there won't be the set-up, the funding, the places, the trained people to support them, to offer them good health-care and accommodation options. And there certainly won't be enough palliative-care centres. There aren't now.'


No doubt exists that if euthanasia were permitted the family of Eva Dilorenzo would have chosen it for her. Would Eva have chosen it and, having chosen, gone through with it? That question stuck in my head like a nail. Nina said that until a week before her death Eva remained hopeful, that she just didn't believe she was dying. When she lost hope, she said she had 'had enough and asked to be drugged'. Did Eva mean she wanted to be put into an unconscious state, or did she mean she wanted be killed? Paul and Nina were very close to Eva, and they have no doubt Eva referred to death.

Eva's request came soon after her admission to McCulloch

House when she was in severe pain and at the point where she had finally accepted the fact she would soon die. A week later Eva was interested enough in life to order a new nightie and have her hair dyed, actions not based on vanity but on values. Being well-groomed was a habit of a lifetime, an issue of pride and self-image. Her life mattered to her, and it mattered that she lived it to the end in a manner that would be part of her grand-daughter's legacy of memories.

For the family, witnessing Eva's pain was intolerable. It is fair to ask whether this influenced how or what they heard. Although they appreciated the care that surrounded both patient and family, they remained bitter about her end. Stopping Eva's pain would also have stopped their pain. It is interesting to note that when a staff member complied with the family's wish to have Eva 'very sedated', it was 'against the grain'. Why would it be 'against the grain' unless it was obvious to the professionals present that the family needed it done as much, or more, than Eva?

The Dilorenzo family arrived at McCulloch House still shaken by the lack of trust and understanding they experienced with the initial diagnostician. His choice of words, 'the horse has already bolted', and his dismissal of their shock and fear—'this isn't a tragedy, the [Tasmanian] massacre's the tragedy'—deeply affected them. Although the precise context of these remarks is unknown, many patients and staff told me of similar experiences and cited doctors' 'poor communication skills'. Medical specialists were often described as 'dismissive' or 'arrogant'. An officious or cold attitude can greatly increase the stress already felt by the severely ill and their family.

Many doctors, perhaps because of their scientific orientation, tend to view patients through the patient's disease, that the patients' lives and bodies exist as objects for the exercise of their professional skills. Others, because of the demanding and sometimes unpleasant nature of their work, distance their feelings from their patients to survive a work atmosphere that can be and often is a cauldron of emotion. Some who are naturally skilled in communicating may refuse to do so when giving bad news to a patient or the patient's family. They are sensitive, they hate causing distress, they are frightened of causing a scene. They know what to do but prefer to skirt the issue and the subsequent burden of a patient's anguish.

One could speculate forever on the reasons why others are poor communicators. In some cases the reasons could be economic. Breaking bad news in an appropriate way is time-consuming and time is money. It is not uncommon for a doctor to have another professional deliver the bad news for them, or they soften the blow with euphemisms. The first choice can leave a patient feeling abandoned just when his or her need for support is greatest; the second choice can result in confusion followed by a sense of bitter betrayal.

Some doctors are aware that their words are weapons. They can affect the hearer like a supportive hug or a slap in the face. Eye contact, a facial expression, body movements or tone of voice tell a story as powerfully as words. Younger doctors appear more aware of this other dimension of communication, as well as acknowledging they have a moral, ethical and human duty to tell patients clearly what is happening to them and what is likely to happen in the future.

The Dilorenzos remained mute in the face of the specialist's diminution of their family tragedy. But they paid dispropor-tionately for their good manners and restraint in terms of enduring lasting anger and humiliation. 'We just had to get away from there,' Nina said. What fear in those words, what a sense of running from something capable of inflicting pain! But what interested me was something beyond my ability to determine. How much did that experience deplete the family's moral strength and help create the feeling of intolerable pressure during Eva's last weeks?

One other element in Eva Dilorenzo's death is noteworthy. When a priest entered Eva's room, the family, daughter-in-law Nina in particular, reacted with anger and resentment. As the family attested, though, the minutes that followed went well. The question, however, is: what has Christianity done that the unexpected sight of one of its representatives inspires spontaneous anger, discomfort and diminishment? Dr Patrick D. Wall, professor of anatomy at University College, London, would likely reply that what Christianity did was to help bar the way to the relief of pain by giving all suffering an automatic moral value.

In *Defeating Pain: The War against a Silent Epidemic*, Dr Wall describes the alleged moral value of pain as 'the most potent and persistent myth' in perpetuating avoidable suffering. 'This belief pervades the whole of our Western culture and is deeply rooted in—and legitimised by—our dominant religion, Christianity. Long after Christianity had become a dominant religion, devout Christians by the score inflicted pain and suffering on themselves in order to raise their moral status.'* Wall points out that while many Christians reject the belief that suffering is necessary and desirable, the belief in its intrinsic moral potential has exerted a profound cultural and intellectual influence.

What *was* the meaning of Eva's suffering? Did it have any meaning? Would it have been better for everyone if Eva had

---

* Patrick D. Wall & Mervyn Jones, *Defeating Pain: The War against a Silent Epidemic*.

been killed with a lytic cocktail—a high flow-rate intravenous injection of a toxic combination of drugs—a week earlier, two weeks earlier, or whenever? What was this agony all about? Nina had said that 'the whole business' had brought the family very close together, but this was a devoted shoulder-to-shoulder family, anyway. How close does a family have to be? Was this all that resulted from Eva's agony?

If this was the answer, it was no use to me at all. I had hoped that as I dug deeper, went further, some answer, some inspiration, or some shred of certitude would take possession of me. I longed to be rid of my uncertainty yet seemed to be getting no closer to the 'right' answer. Maybe, I thought, I am not going to find one. Maybe there is no such thing.

# Living Fully until Death

*The value of life lies not in the length of days but in the use you make of them; he has lived for a long time who has little lived. Whether you have lived enough depends not on the number of your years but on your will.*
—Montaigne, *Essays*

O n several afternoons at McCulloch House I see the same threesome in the lounge: a tall, slim, fair-haired woman in her late forties, an athletic young woman with long, glossy brown hair and an infrequent smile—obviously her daughter—and a merry, full-figured woman, who lacks the bossiness of a sister but has the authority of a friend. Laughter characterises the exchange between the two older women, but the younger one shows little inclination to join in. The fair-haired woman's name is Yvonne Linden, her daughter is Gillian (Jill), and the cheerful companion is Rose Benson.

'I suppose you want to know how old I am,' Yvonne says to me when we finally meet. Her air is friendly, crisp, and nicely feisty. 'I'm fifty, and that's probably as old as I'm ever going to be. No complaints, though. I've had a lot more time than I expected to have.'

Yvonne explains that she had radical surgery for ovarian cancer six years earlier. A nurse by profession, she worked at Dandenong Hospital for twenty-seven years and wasn't involved with ovarian cancer patients. She 'never dreamed' of getting it, something she now regards as 'really dumb', and went to pieces when she found out.

'I was a mess. I was crazy. I drove my husband so mad he couldn't take it. He just took off. Went to Germany and stayed there a few weeks. I think you could say I didn't handle it very well.'

At this point Yvonne laughs and hugs her daughter, Jill, who begins to cry silently, hopelessly. But Yvonne won't let her cry. 'Come on, come on, enough of that, sweetie.' With her arm across her daughter's shoulder, Yvonne continues her story. I suggest she start at the beginning.

'You mean when I was young, married, that sort of thing?' A smile slides over her face. 'I went to a convent, the Notre Dame de Sion nuns at Box Hill. Oh, boy, they were the days! I smiled once at a boy in chapel, and one of the nuns told me I was "the most boy-minded girl in the school".'

Yvonne hoots with laughter and then leans back against the thick pink roses of the chintz couch. I tell her she probably was, that the nuns were expert at spotting decadent tendencies. Jill rewards me with a weak, grateful smile, and Yvonne lightly slaps me on the knee.

While Yvonne was training at Austin Hospital she met her husband, Kurt. With a group of student nurses she went to the Ski Club, the dance hall next to where the old St Moritz skating rink used to be in St Kilda. They married, moved to Dandenong, bought their first house, had a son, went on a world cruise, and lived for a couple of years in South Africa, where Yvonne worked as a nurse in a factory. When they returned home she resumed nursing.

'I married at twenty-one. Made the right choice. Our son's twenty-seven, and Jill here is twenty-two, married now to a real sweetheart, Craig. Then in 1991, out of the blue, I had this terrible haemorrhage and doctors found a tumour on the ovary. Until then I'd never really thought about life and death. I simply took life as it came. But then I'd been lucky. I'd never lost anyone, just my husband's mother.

'I went back to work after surgery. The way things go—you know, you learn a new word and then you see it a dozen times in a week—well, after surgery I came into a lot of contact with ovarian cancer at work. The doctor didn't keep up a bluff front, thank heavens, but my family and friends did. I didn't think that my surgery had gotten everything. I knew what it was going to do and no one could tell me otherwise. I wasn't being an old killjoy. I could see what it did every day at work. After a while they all knew better than to argue with me.'

Two years after Yvonne's surgery Kurt was diagnosed with cancer in the colon and lymph glands, which was treated with chemotherapy and surgery. At this point in her story Yvonne pauses. She is an easy talker, so I sense she isn't searching for the right words to say but for the meaning of those words. She wants something recorded, not because she is hurt or mystified by it, but because it conveys something she hasn't yet come to terms with.

'I think I've given Kurt more support than he's given me. I'm not saying that for any reason other than it's a fact. Dad [Kurt] has just not been able to give it. He's not articulate. He's a deep thinker, very quiet. I want to tell you this, although I'm not sure why, but I want to tell you. The other night I was lying in bed here and I said, "I'm dying you know, Kurt." And he said, "But what will *I* do? What's going to happen to me?"'

At this point Jill again moves into her mother's arms and weeps. Once more Yvonne pressures her with bright words and teasing to stop her grief. Yvonne's refusal to let Jill mourn disturbs me. When Yvonne was young, the keeping up of appearances counted. Character emerged when grief and pain struck and was made evident by a consistently stiff upper lip. Is this part of that old tradition, or is Jill's expression of pain more than Yvonne can bear?

Then Yvonne's parents arrive, both elegant in their eighties, tall and straight, staying side by side as if either, without the other, might topple over from the sheer weight of their imminent loss.

I take my leave and wait until the next day to continue our conversation. I find Yvonne in her room, sitting in a big armchair, buffing her well-manicured, unvarnished nails as she waits to go home. She has no pain whatsoever and eagerly anticipates getting back into her own place. She picks up the conversation from where we left off. It is clear to me that this is a story she wishes to finish, perhaps in the hope of understanding it.

'Kurt's sixty, ten years older. Initially the surgeon said he was very concerned, but Kurt's in his third year now and doing well. One day he asked me for two Panadol. That's how it started. He doesn't like taking any medication, but soon after he asked for two more. He said he had pain in his lower abdomen. I felt we had to investigate it. The doctor palpated his intestinal area, looked him in the face, and said, "It will be cancer."'

After chemotherapy and surgery, Kurt went on a seven-month course of Chinese herbs. Yvonne felt she showed a lot of strength during this period, unlike her initial reaction to her own illness. This support really helped her husband. Personally she was experiencing a major shift in her own interior thinking.

For the first time she sensed her life as transitory, not a permanency at all, not a reality, but something she was simply travelling through. She started to see death as 'just part of life, nothing really special, just part of it'.

Now she tells me, 'I've kept working as a nurse until recently. I've always been a compassionate, good nurse—understanding and a good listener. I took time out for chemotherapy, and then a second stop for another tumour on the groin, and then on the liver. Chemotherapy has been offered again, but I've been through that.'

Yvonne says the loss of her hair was extremely difficult to cope with. Well-groomed hair was a point of pride with her, a factor central to her sense of well-being. She lost it once, and now that it has grown back intends to keep it. Despite her illness it is still thick, fair, healthy. She notices I am gazing at her hair, then looks at me with eyes that suddenly fill with tears. Flicking a tissue from the box on the bedside table, she pulls herself together. 'I've been offered chemo, but I've refused. I had an ultrasound at the hospital yesterday, and the cancer's all over my liver.'

She glances past me into the garden, thinking aloud. 'I've had enough. I've been through it all. Enough's enough. My family has to get on with their lives. It's going to take me soon, regardless of whether I have chemo or not. We've got to accept that. We've got to be practical and not beat around the bush.'

Jill has arrived to accompany her mother home. Urgently, as if she is repeating that day's lesson and is struggling to set her will on it, she says, 'Mum, I do accept it. I do accept what's happening.' I feel Jill is being coaxed into a position of strength and cheerfulness when all she really wants to do is cry her eyes out. If Jill isn't allowed to grieve, are Yvonne's parents? The chance to pursue this question doesn't come until two weeks later.

Within ten days of her happy, brave departure Yvonne is readmitted to McCulloch House with multiple symptoms. She is in pain, restless, nauseous and profoundly depressed. The door of her room remains closed. She doesn't want to see anybody. The staff tells me about her condition, and I make no attempt to see her. Her life has entered its final stage. For months she succeeded intellectually in facing the inevitable. Now she is facing it emotionally. For three days her door remains shut while she fights the last real battle of her life.

Then one morning she emerges from her room, thinner, tired, totally pain-free, and ready to live just a little more, have a few more laughs, spread a little more love.

'What is it with men?' she asks as we sit outside in the garden for some golden autumn sunlight. 'I told you Kurt was the right choice for me. It's been good. But there I was the other night, the biggest psychological mess you ever saw and he said, not once but twice, "But I want you to get old with me. What am I going to do?"' For a few moments she is silent, then gives a deep sigh. 'We've been together nearly thirty years. It's Kurt's way of saying how much he'll miss me.' Another silence then a wry laugh. 'It'd help if he'd find another way to say it, but that's men for you.'

We sit in silence for a while and then I ask about her parents. Yvonne replies that she has been so busy with her husband, son and daughter that only in the past few days has she realised she had left them out of the picture, taking it for granted that they could cope.

'They're in their eighties. Even though I'm fifty and dying, I still feel like I'm the child and they're my parents and somehow in charge. We never get out of that role, not unless we're forced to. But in the past few days I've been thinking differently. I wasn't cold. I haven't left them out deliberately. Maybe I've even been trying to protect them. My God, why can't I answer that? I cut them out of so much of what's been happening. I've left them to handle it themselves!'

This realisation of time's ability to reverse roles affects Yvonne deeply. She now sees her parents as two human beings who have to cope not only with her decline, but the inescapable fact that they are close to their own end, and might soon be separated one from the other after a lifetime together. She is puzzled by why it has taken her own death to see her mother and father as people, not just as parents.

Her view towards her daughter's grieving has changed too. She is aware of the importance of letting Jill fully express her grief while she is still there to share it with her.

I ask Yvonne what she hopes will come from our talks. She doesn't hesitate to reply, 'I'd like you to tell the world about this place. I'm a nurse and I didn't know what palliative care really was, what could be done just so people could die peacefully. This continuous offering of treatment when we know there is no hope…it's so wrong. This is what we've been taught in the medical profession, that technology is our saviour, that we should save people at all costs. It leads to hopeless interventions with people near death and only adds to their suffering. It surrounds everything with secrecy so that nobody really knows what's happening to them.'

'What do you mean by secrecy?' I ask.

'Most people are very frightened of death, so these things feed into one another. It suits hospitals, the medical profession, that people are so frightened of dying. Nobody knows then what's really happening to them and the medical profession can go on acting as if it has something to offer, intervening with surgery and God knows what, when everyone knows there's no hope. People are afraid to ask, to find out what goes on.'

I interrupt to ask, 'But just what does go on?'

Yvonne laughs shortly. 'We'd be here forever if I started in on that. Well, I've seen surgery done on a ninety-two-year-old man, not to relieve pain, but to give him more "time". A week or two more! At ninety-two, and all of it spent in post-surgical pain! Don't think the idiocy is limited to dramatic cases like that one. It goes on all the time—blood transfusions, shots, surgeries, trying this drug, trying that, all on people who can't possibly recover and whose poor bodies are simply being tortured by all this. Death's just part of life. Why can't we start looking it in the face and work at making dying better instead of pretending things can be turned around?'

This isn't a question as much as a despairing observation, and it gives me an opening to ask about euthanasia.

'I'm a Christian and I'm going to be with God,' Yvonne says. 'I truly believe that. Although I went to the convent, I have no religion, no specific faith, nothing. Yet I feel God will accept me.' After a pause, she continues. 'I would believe in euthanasia for myself, for my family's sake. Yes, for my family's sake I would.' Then she adds, 'The family just has to get on with its life.'

Kurt, however, doesn't share this view. 'I'm not keen about euthanasia,' he tells me in the only conversation we have. 'I feel if they bring a law out the kids can get rid of you at a certain age. If someone wants to take his life, you can get yourself out of the way, anyway. Personally I'd never do it and I'd never bring a law out so you could kill yourself.'

Not long after my last conversation with Yvonne, Jill and Yvonne's close friend, Rose Benson, were sleeping at McCulloch House in the overnight guest room when a nurse woke them in the early hours of the morning.

'We went down to Mum's room,' Jill tells me later. 'It was four in the morning. I was trying to give Mum a cuddle and a kiss and tell her I loved her when she sat up in bed. I couldn't believe it. She was completely aware and immediately tried to cheer me up. She said, "Let's all sing a happy song together." I can't remember the name. What was it? A happy, happy song, popular, well known. Why can't I remember? We all sang it, Mum, too, and then she lay back down and died.'

After a moment of silence, Jill says, 'Mum spent her last days seeing everyone. She wasn't really being philosophic. She just wanted everyone to know she'd had a wonderful life and she wanted to tell everybody she thought the world of them. She wanted to know that we'd be all OK. She wanted to give everyone strength.' She interrupts herself in order to control her voice. 'I could face anything, anything in the world because of Mum, because of the courage she gave me.'

Dr Lesley Cadzow, thirty-eight, married, and now on the staff at McCulloch House, trained in general practice in Glasgow. For weeks I have been trying to pin Lesley down for an interview, and now that I have done so, I hustle her into the private recessed sitting area at the end of the main wing, fearful that any moment a nurse will spot her and haul her away.

Lesley's expertise at calling a spade a spade is matched by a feminine, warm and culturally uninhibited approach to the problems of patients. I ask her about her background and she tells me that she and her husband, a microbiologist, emigrated to New Zealand where she was appointed as paediatric registrar in a hospital. They later moved on to Australia. With a mind and a heart entirely focused on freeing patients from any suffering attached to dying, she thinks McCulloch House is an excellent palliative care centre, but not as creative as it could be.

'My own mother died of liver disease when she was sixty-eight and that heightens your consciousness,' she says. 'You get into a big hospital like she was in Glasgow and you lose. The buildings, strangers, the medical atmosphere are the antithesis of the rage, grief, mystery, sorrow, rituals, celebration of a life just ending.'

Lesley then tells of a patient who didn't 'lose', a ballroom-dancing teacher who lived at Mentone, a suburb of Melbourne, and was cared for by her teenage son when she fell ill. She died on Christmas Day. When Lesley was told her patient was critical, she and a couple of friends left their Christmas dinner and went to her. Lesley knew her patient would want to go out with a bang. They all got into bed with her, propping her up, holding her, and celebrating Christmas. The patient, Lesley says with a big smile, had 'a lovely, celebratory death'.

She insists 'there's no reason why most people can't have such deaths. We don't encourage families to do enough, to massage feet, to clean mouths, to put on make-up, to celebrate lives. Not even here. Other people, strangers, take over, and that diminishes the family involvement. Even here people don't have as much choice as they should. That's one of the reasons I'm here, to bring a degree of change. Michael [Ashby] knows that.

'It distresses me when someone could go home and they can't because, well, maybe the family is too frightened. In Scotland many people die at home. Here, medically, we seem to have lost the ability to tell people what the reality is. We don't seem to be able to say, "If you do this, this will happen, and if you do that, that will happen." In hospitals there are countless interventions. It's a natural push in an active, dynamic hospital to try this, do that, but I'm not a strong advocate of that approach at all.'

I ask Lesley what helped form her views. She speaks again of her experiences with her mother in Glasgow, her work in New Zealand, and remarks that being stationed for six months in Alice Springs with the Flying Doctor Service gave her an understanding of the powerful role the community can play in death.

'I spent six weeks on Bathurst Island in the Aboriginal community during that time. There was a frail, debilitated woman, an old sixty-five, with pneumonia and chest pains. She had a huge extended family. They wanted treatment for her, but they would never follow up. We kept suggesting things, comforting things, but all they wanted her to have was an antibiotic.

'She lay on the verandah of a three-room government house, a place with a tin of sugar, a couple of tea bags and a means of boiling water. There was a gambling school over the way with bets up to $2000, and children going back and forth over the verandah, and dogs running around.

'The woman lay on a dirty sheet on a dirty mattress. Everyone would sit around and hold her and pat her back. There's a strong church group there, and there were a few crosses scattered around, and a Virgin, plus Aboriginal songs, and one girl playing a guitar now and then. They sang really beautifully.

'The women sat closer in, the men sat further away. The family would give her a drink, but they did the bare minimum. We kept suggesting things, but they never followed through. In a tribal system you can't get close enough to touch someone dying. Everyone else is too close around them.'

Lesley says there were many seeming contradictions in the community's behaviour—the asking for treatment but not following through, the giving only of water but the constancy of attention and love. It took her a while to understand what was really happening.

'The tribe perceived me as doing active euthanasia, whereas they, in fact, were doing passive euthanasia, just letting nature take its course. They wanted me there to verify what they thought. Finally they said she was dead. No one touched her. We had to wash her and wrap her up into the sheet. Then all the men dressed up. They put on white ochre and red loincloths and ran white ochre through their hair and stuck cockatoo feathers into it.

'We carried the woman into an ambulance and drove no more than a few minutes away. Somehow a bed appeared there, outside, with a clean new mattress. We placed her on it and then the men moved around it, beating their chests, screaming, and hitting themselves with sticks. She had her own burial plot with a *pukumani* pole, beautifully painted with an intricate design. The whole ritual was community-involved, expressive, and full of meaning.'

This community involvement in a member's death deeply impressed her, contrasting painfully with the tendency hospitals had 'to treat people like children because they are in pyjamas'. The doctor–patient relationship, she says, should be a two-way street.

'We need their skills. It's very important for our patients to know that.' There is an urgency in Lesley's voice, a flavour of the advocate who has seen great injustice. 'These people have had full lives. Many of them are very clever, brilliant in business or academics, or in managing and negotiating diffi-cult family relations. We're just on the edge of knowledge.

We need the input of the patient.

'You know what haunts me? The screams of a child being taken to the cancer treatment centre. Yes, I'm haunted by that. I've heard it. Why don't we use hypnosis? It can help the brain absent itself when there's something traumatic and dreadful. What stops us from using it? I'm an acupuncturist, but we don't use acupuncture here. Why not?'

Slightly exasperated, Lesley sighs. 'Michael knows my feelings on this. With a few people, alternative medicine—diet, meditation, inner strength—works. We *know* the close bridge between mind and body. Why don't we at least *try* these things?'


Yvonne Linden died fully human, fully alive, absorbed in an awareness of others to her final moment. Her last act was one of will, designed to leave a memory bright and spirited enough to warm a generation of grandchildren she would never see.

When her desire to live—revealed in her going 'crazy' at her diagnosis—met her equally powerful respect for reality, reality won. Yvonne bit the bullet, accepted her fate, and went on working as a 'compassionate, loving' nurse. In her desire to set an example of courage, she came close to making a terrible mistake: she refused to let others openly express their grief at her approaching death. The freedom to express one's grief prior to death—anticipatory grief—is believed by grief counsellors to help shorten the time of mourning and readjustment.

When I first spoke to Yvonne, she was totally confident she had accepted her fate. This confidence reinforced her ability to keep cheering others up that, in effect, denied them any opportunity to express their sorrow. Whenever Jill cried, Yvonne instantly, lovingly, shushed her up.

After Yvonne returned to McCulloch House, she went

through a final, private crisis. She had faced her death for years, but this, as is the case with many anticipated deaths, had been essentially a theoretical facing. Now it was nearby, real, inescapable. When I met Yvonne after she went through this final crisis of physical, emotional, and spiritual pain, she had broken through into a state of intense awareness. Was she ready for death? Probably not. She was only fifty, still full of fun. She had a husband, two bright young adult children, a home she loved, and a career to which she was devoted. Ready? Probably not. But she now understood the importance of allowing her family and friends to express their grief fully so that its burden, shared by everyone, would be lightened. She realised her death was not hers alone, that when she died she would take slices of their lives with her. Hers was a community death with family, relatives, friends, co-workers. She moved to bring her parents fully into her life and opened the door to every recess in her heart. In doing so she experienced the rich cycle of life, child now consoling parents, son and daughter consoling mother. This sense of wholeness and completion, although painful, brought Yvonne profound peace. She chose to look at her husband's statements—not unusual when the wife dies first—as a recognition of her value and uniqueness, not an outburst of masculine egotism.

In the last days of her life she asked me repeatedly to tell others that 'there is nothing to be afraid of in death. Death is part of life.' She spoke of the misery suffered because of fear and denial of death, of patients partially cooked with radiation, sick with toxic chemicals, uncomfortable, exhausted, spending their last weeks, not enjoying peace and making some sense of their life, or saying their last goodbyes, but struggling to score and win in a no-win situation.

Yvonne had told me that when she learned of her disease

she was thrown into chaos, yet I could see that the closer she came to death the greater became her personal creative powers. Her sense of the naturalness of death, her consciousness of life, her insight into others' needs, invested this process with a sense akin to adventure. Rather than a courageous resignation in the face of death, Yvonne now seemed to consent almost joyously.

A great deal changed between the Yvonne who went 'crazy' and the Yvonne who led a song moments before she died. The question is: what was behind this change? Or was it not change as much as giving full play to previously untapped aspects of her interior life? She said she believed in euthanasia *for her family's sake*. Was this a theoretical belief? Despite the illegality of euthanasia, occasionally a patient or family asks for it. Yvonne did not, even though she suffered pain.

What did all this mean for me? Yvonne worked hard in her life to be caring and compassionate and she died that way. She lived to the hilt because she understood she had work to do with her family, lessons to teach, gifts to give, perhaps even a faith to reveal. She felt no one else could do it quite as she could do it. She had had a full life, wanted to pick its fruits, and hand them out before she left. She had learned wisdom by being at the bottom of the pit.

Her words—that she would accept euthanasia *for her family's sake so they could get on with their lives*—strengthened my perception that if the state sanctions euthanasia, won't many older people who are terminally ill feel under severe pressure to ask for it simply *for the family's sake?*

# Attitude

*Let knowledge grow from more to more,*
*But more of reverence in us dwell;*
*That mind and soul, according well,*
*May make one music as before.*
   —Lord Alfred Tennyson, 'In Memoriam A. H. H.'

As the weeks pass, I become more 'at home' with death, although no closer to resolving my central problem than when I started. So many questions, on so many levels, surround the end of life that at times I find myself less focused on palliative care and euthanasia than on the broader topic of life and suffering.

Ironically, because I know no place more serene, protective and comfortable than McCulloch House, it is the writings of Viktor Frankl that most often come to mind. Frankl, a Viennese psychiatrist, survived four years in Auschwitz and other concentration camps. During this time his entire family, except for one sister, was executed. After the war, Frankl wrote *Man's Search for Meaning*, a book in which he said, among other things, that what was really needed was a fundamental change in our attitude towards life. We had to learn that 'it didn't really matter what we expected from life, but rather what life expected from us.'*

When I first read these words decades earlier, I had taken it for granted that the unspeakable conditions of Auschwitz had shaped Frankl's harsh view of life. I had brashly thought his philosophy reminiscent of the old-fashioned sermons I had heard in church on the moral gains to be made from suffering. Since then—since I was a correspondent in Vietnam, Laos and Cambodia during the Vietnam War; since being a visitor in peaceful, prosperous Yugoslavia just before the bloodbath started; since being a reporter in Beijing before the government killed some of its finest youth like a farmer slaughtering chickens; since all these experiences and watching the events in Northern Ireland, Rwanda, and a half-dozen other blood-soaked countries; since everything that has happened in my own personal life—I have accepted Frankl's statement as the central truth of reality. Whatever the millions of men, women and children of those places expected from life had absolutely no relationship to what they got.

From such a grinding-down by reality in Auschwitz, Frankl concluded—and he was referring to *unavoidable* suffering—that when a person found that it was his destiny to suffer he had to accept suffering as his 'single and unique task'. Suffering became a work, a monumental labour of mind, heart and will. Suffering had to be entered into, embraced and re-perceived. The chance to discover what life means, Frankl said, lies in our acceptance of suffering, deprivation and loss. But this doesn't involve the relinquishment of hope. Just as hope is necessary to the terminally ill, so Auschwitz prisoners hoped for small mercies—that their swollen feet would still get into their

* Viktor Frankl, *Man's Search for Meaning: An Introduction to Logotherapy.*

sodden, paper-thin shoes, or that there might be some peas in their daily ration of watery soup.

What did Frankl mean about forgetting our expectations from life when faced with unavoidable suffering? I believe he meant a willingness to open our hearts to a complete conversion. 'Conversion' is a tricky word, smacking as it does of bible-belt evangelism. By it I mean a profound psychic shift, less a willingness to change than a willingness to look, *in an entirely different manner*, at what has always been present within us and what we are currently experiencing. In this case it would call for the letting go of all one's own expectations of life and focusing on life's—until then hidden within—expectations of us.

Not everyone can accomplish this feat, nor would they want to. And certainly not everyone is 'called' to do it. But what has become clear to me is that some people *are* 'called'. I don't know by whom, or what, or why, but fate does seem to set them up, courtesy of their genes, a virus, or whatever. Those persons who can embrace their fate are able to make even an ordinary life into a unique, sometimes powerful, statement that imprints its image on the heart of every person close to them.

To raise the question of attitude in the face of the agony some terminally ill patients endure is a risky thing to do, since it could be misread as a suggestion that sufferers asking for euthanasia simply lack 'the right attitude'. However, and this needs to be stressed, the question of attitude is important because it is part of *everyone's* psychological state—the patient, the patient's family and the patient's friends.

It is the medical profession's attitude towards the use of opioids and people's general attitude towards death and dying that is responsible for most of the unnecessary pain that accompanies dying today. Attitude touches directly on the factors that go into the decision to opt, theoretically, for euthanasia or to reject it, theoretically. Numerous studies have indicated a relationship between state of mind—depression, agitation, guilt, worry—and sensitivity to the intensity of pain experienced.

Some patients who suffer intensely don't want euthanasia, and it is by no means adherence to a religious faith that always determines this decision. People's individuality, uniqueness, family history, experiences, and education all go into making the decisions they take, including the way in which they choose to die. The attitude they adopt towards their own suffering—whether or not they can intuitively do what Frankl suggests and make it into their work—can have an effect on the way they die. Because most of us are members of a family 'community' the results can be transgenerational, adding to family mythology and providing an example, for good or bad, for years to come. What better proof of this than Viktor Frankl himself?

Adrian Rhys-Mendoza, who died in March 1997, aged thirty-six, was one McCulloch House patient with an attitude in spades. Adrian was the youngest child, and only boy, of four children born to Diane and Richard Rhys-Mendoza in Sri Lanka. The family lived well in Colombo, but when political troubles started in the early 1970s they moved to Australia. The adjustment was difficult, particularly for the women. The move not only involved a different culture but the substitution of a large house with servants for a small flat, no household help, trains instead of a chauffeured car, and a job search.

Adrian, twelve at the time, had attended an international school and settled into Melbourne with little difficulty. The family was outgoing, athletic and well-educated. The three girls—Carol, Helen and Paige—were fine young swimmers.

They all taught for the Victorian Swimming Association and eventually all three married.

Adrian was also athletic. He swam, played tennis, was captain of his lacrosse team and was a volunteer lifesaver. At seventeen he fell ill with Hodgkin's disease, a malignant progressive condition marked by enlargement of the lymph nodes, spleen and liver. Its cause is unknown. The prognosis was a death sentence. The only question was when the disease would take his life. Shock and grief swept through the large Rhys-Mendoza clan.

Adrian reacted badly to chemotherapy and radiotherapy. A strong, healthy, ebullient teenager with his whole life ahead of him, he turned overnight into a nauseated, vomiting patient with a terminal illness. But as time passed and the disease gave no evidence of its presence, Adrian believed himself to be cured. Or did he? In any case, Adrian's attitude was that of a young man with a long and full life spread before him.

He married at twenty-one and was divorced by twenty-three. He never remarried. He joined television's Channel 7 and became manager of the sports division, travelling overseas for events. He was a member of the Helicopter Rescue Squad, and a world traveller in brief, busy vacations. In 1994 he accepted a job in Delhi, India, as general manager of an advertising agency project. Two years later the project was completed. However, the disease he had evaded for years was now creeping up on him. Bouts of sickness and fatigue were accompanied by some difficulty in movement. He longed to explore Europe, do everything he wanted to do, and go everywhere he wanted to go. After three months in Europe, and increasing disability, he returned via Sri Lanka to Australia.

'I started a quest for a cure when Adrian was diagnosed at seventeen,' Diane, his mother, says to me one day at McCulloch

House. She is a vital, stylish woman with a fine direct manner. 'I stormed heaven for a healing. I had been raised as an Anglican but converted to Catholicism when Adrian had his first bout of illness. I wanted to find a church that was open all day and the Catholic church was. I believed in miracles. I see this now as immature, but that's what I'd read into the faith.'

Diane says that although Adrian practised no religion, he was open to a spiritual life. 'He went to Sri Lanka to search for what we call "the healing light". I met him there, and when I saw him I knew his condition was irreparable. He could barely put one foot in front of the other. He came home here to East Malvern to live with me. He wanted no more chemo or radio-therapy, only alternative medicine—Chinese herbs, shiatsu massage, homeopathic treatments. He was rapidly losing weight and this worried me terribly. He told me, "Mum, I'm thirty-five years old. Please don't interfere with my illness. I know my body."'

Diane and Adrian's father, Richard, divorced in 1980, but Richard and the whole family now pulled together. Adrian's former boss from Channel 7 also spent time with Adrian daily.

'I went on hoping for a miracle,' Diane says. 'I kept my mind on what belief could do. It gave me all the strength I needed. It kept me focused, helped me keep my composure. Without belief my sadness would have added terribly to Adrian's burden.'

After a long decline, Adrian was first admitted to Royal Melbourne Hospital and then later to McCulloch House. He must have been in severe distress to have qualified for accep-tance at McCulloch House, but Diane admits she didn't know whether he was or not. Throwing up her hands in mixed bewil-derment and admiration, she says, 'He would never, never say if he was in pain. Whenever he spoke to the doctor, he insisted

I leave the room. He wanted the truth and they gave it to him. Paige, my daughter, and I fought a lot about this. She wanted to know the exact medical prognosis, and all I wanted was a miracle. I didn't want to hear the other.

'Adrian kept losing weight, forty kilos by then instead of his usual eighty. He didn't see himself as a victim, although occasionally he was a little depressed. One time he cried, but it wasn't for himself. A five-year-old Aboriginal boy in Queensland had been set on fire in a school ground by a lunatic. Adrian had just seen the story on television and it broke his heart. As he wept, he said, "Oh, Mum, I am not as strong as him, not nearly as strong as that poor child." He didn't care for pious talk, but he believed in himself and a higher power. He drew his incredible strength from this belief, drew his ability to remain cheerful, make jokes and be funny and pleasant to the end.'

On a Friday night three weeks after Adrian's admission to McCulloch House, Mario, a resident in internal medicine who was doing a three-week stint in palliative care, sought Diane out and drew her to the lounge. Sitting down with her, he said, 'He's slowly dying, Diane. There isn't much time.' After all those years of knowing, Diane flatly denied it and felt a rush of fearful anger at Mario's prognosis. She *knew* she would still have her miracle. That night Adrian's nephew, Terence, as close to him as a brother, was expected from Queensland.

'I went to Adrian and sat beside him,' Diane says now. 'He said to me, "I'm going, Mum. I can't hold on." I said, "But Terence's plane is just landing. Hold on. Terence is in a cab. Hold on. He's driving along Dandenong Road. Hold on. He'll soon be here." Shortly after, Terence arrived.'

That evening Diane moved a bed into Adrian's room and stayed there until the end. She remained unshaken in her conviction that nineteen years of prayer would be rewarded with a miracle, that Adrian would suddenly recover and the disease would go into permanent remission. Her mind-set distressed the staff who, while well aware of Diane's beliefs, felt it essential to prepare her for Adrian's imminent death. 'We were torn in two,' one nurse said. 'We wanted her to accept the truth of what was about to happen, but we never force the truth on someone who has chosen not to hear it.'

The following day Peter [Martin] sat Diane down and tried to prepare her. 'Diane, we're only giving Adrian a few hours.' Diane looked at Peter as she had at Mario, angry and rejecting. No, God wouldn't betray her. She would tolerate no suggestion of that. Later that Saturday, Adrian bounced back, his body emaciated, his mind sharp, his attitude upbeat. From under his pillow he pulled out a stack of travel folders and started perusing them as if planning a holiday.

He had been expected to die on the Friday night, but on Tuesday he received five sets of visitors in the lounge. With staff help he had maintained all his personal grooming rituals—daily bath, thick black hair shampooed and shining, nails trimmed and clean. When he was wheeled back to his room, he phoned all his friends around the world. He chatted, joked, and then, assuring them they shouldn't worry or grieve, he affectionately said goodbye, explaining he was dying. Late that night Adrian started to fight for breath. His whole family, including nephews and nieces, surrounded his bed. His death was ordinary— shivering, sweat, a long battle for breath and an increase in morphine to relieve the pain of the struggle and to mitigate any growing fear. He died in the early morning.

The length of Adrian's illness left his relatives totally exhausted at his death. Although profound grief was the common cause, each family member experienced it in a slightly different way. Diane's reaction was a realisation of her own spiritual immaturity. 'The scales fell from my eyes the day Adrian died. I decided to let my feelings come out. "Where are you, God? Where are you? What were all my prayers for? What was my faith all about?" I was angry, deeply angry. I knew nothing worse could happen to me.'

Some time later I visit Diane and two of her daughters—Helen and Paige—at her home. In the living room a framed picture of Adrian sits on a corner table. Two vases, each containing a small bunch of flowers, sit either side of the photograph.

Helen, like all the girls, had adored her 'baby' brother. 'Since his death,' she says, 'I've felt nothing—as if I'm living in a vacuum. I've got three children and I feel totally wiped out. If I could have talked to Adrian about it, it might have been better. But he didn't want to talk about himself. Always it was about Mum. "How is Mum. How is she doing, really?" That's what dominated his concerns.' She laughs and tells me he never asked how *she* was doing, then adds, 'We have to get through this, have to let our grief run its course.'

Paige, on the other hand, admits, 'I could talk to my kids about it but not to my husband. With something like this, you forget how to be happy. You don't know how to be fun. I'd felt so flat for so long. I came home after he died. I had been so strong all day because we had to make the funeral arrangements and all the phone calls. I went home and then I started shaking. I couldn't stop it. My husband asked, "Why are you shaking?" I replied, "Why do you think I'm shaking?"'

I look at all three women in turn. 'Did Adrian ever consider killing himself, or did he ask for euthanasia?'

There is a jolting silence, then a murmur of fervent nos. After another pause Diane speaks up. 'When Adrian died, I lost my most precious possession. My heart broke into a thousand pieces like a jigsaw puzzle. I can see now how immature I was in my faith. One day recently I ran into a friend at church who had lost a nineteen-year-old daughter. He told me how happy he was to see me, that his own wife would never trust God or set foot in a church again. When he said that, I felt someone had driven a knife in my heart. I could see the wife's despair, but the pain of her closing up her heart was worse. At that moment I had a sense of a picture that was coming together, slowly, bit by bit, like a jigsaw puzzle. It might take years. I don't know what the picture will look like, but whatever it is, pain has opened me up to receive it.'

Adrian had asked to be cremated and his ashes taken back to Colombo. On 4 July the Rhys-Mendoza family flew to Sri Lanka, buried some of Adrian's ashes in his grandfather's grave, and held a memorial service at St Thomas College, in Mount Lavinia. Since his death, Adrian's personality has continued to send reverberations throughout his family, invading their daydreams and their sleep at night.

'Adrian first appeared to Terence,' Diane tells me two months after our initial meeting. 'Terence had always been like his small brother. Adrian ran into his room dressed in a T-shirt and long tight shorts, and took Terence by the hand, ran with him down the street, and led him to a large house set in a big garden. Standing there in his usual stance with his arms outstretched as if he owned the world, he said, "Look at this!" That was one of his favourite expressions. Then he appeared to my mum, dressed in similar attire, with his hair bouncing around, but this time he was behind a grille in a lovely green garden. He also appeared to Helen in a new house that was in the process of being built. I was there, in the kitchen, cooking! In all these dreams he was healthy, happy, full of life.'

'How do you interpret all that?' I ask.

'If I interpret these dreams according to my imagination, I'm convinced that God is one thing, and that is love. Also, that there is another life for us, but that life is according to what we believe. Adrian was an eternal optimist. He had large dreams for himself and he constantly hammered those dreams into the minds of his nieces and nephews. There have been shifts in the family, all good, all positive, so much so that my children have said, "Mum, this must be Adrian working for us." His upbeat attitude seems to have infected all of us. He has gone, but I feel he has only gone from our sight.'


Sandra has a cubbyhole of an office by the broad staircase in the original building at McCulloch House. It is the perfect spot for an intimate chat. Although the few pieces of furniture are utilitarian, the cosy cluttered effect is welcoming and comfortable. Sandra is a soft-spoken blonde in her early fifties. The mother of three adult children, she is a half-time pastoral-care worker. Sandra believes pastoral care should be an intrinsic part of palliative care but says it is often not regarded as such nor budgeted for. Trained originally as a medical laboratory technician, she has been faced with psychologically stretching situations throughout her adult life. These experiences have given her profound respect for the uniqueness of others and a deep belief that the spiritual journey is a highly individual matter.

'I have had to learn not to impose my spiritual values on others,' she says. 'People who come to us have been down a long road already. Their integrity means they will die as they have lived. But in every case, I do know that here is a spiritual human being with a vital story to tell.

'Pastoral care isn't concerned with offering answers or even interpreting people's experiences, but in helping people do that for themselves. It is in uncovering the meaning of these experiences that people find their own truths. It's not saying, "Here is God," but simply listening for the pointers of a spiritual experience as people talk, and perhaps asking, "What have you learned from that?" Many people are simply satisfied to find out at the end that life does have a spiritual meaning.'

'How do you make contact with patients in view of so many people's antipathy to things religious?' I ask.

'After a person is admitted, and their pain has been brought under control, and they're feeling better, I go in and introduce myself. I tell them I'm the pastoral-care worker. There's a resonance to the word *pastoral*, and I get some amusing responses. One man asked, "Does that have something to do with farming?" I tell them that McCulloch House is completely non-denominational and I'm there to give support only if they ask for it.

'If people want to receive the sacraments of the church, the ritual, their priest, I arrange that for them. Often, though, there is a background of painful experiences and they don't feel they want any more contact with the church. I hear those stories with sadness and a profound sense of how we can fail one another. On the other hand, there are stories of real reconciliation and healing of the spirit. It's very individual—there are so many elements in a person's life we simply can't know about.

'Pastoral care is about listening to people's stories,' Sandra tells me. 'They are wonderful to hear. People tell me what has made their life worth living, as well as what has caused them pain. I suppose my own experiences of loss and grief, as well as my mistakes and failures, are what I draw on when listening to others. My first husband died when our three children were eight, twelve and fifteen. It sounds absurd, but I just didn't believe that such a thing could happen to us. I had always felt so safe, so secure. It was a life-changing event and brought about a time of real suffering.

'I'm a churchgoer, an Anglican, and always needed to belong to a community. I like the ritual, the symbols, and I want to know people care for me, and I for them. After a time, I became very interested in the idea of pastoral care, having received so much myself, and eventually received a grant that allowed me to undertake a clinical pastoral-education course at the Cancer Institute in Melbourne.'

For Sandra the course was a watershed experience. 'It opened all my senses and I recognised a strong sense of vocation, though not to be ordained. For several years I worked as a facilitator in a community-based psychosocial rehabilitation program, and it was there that I came to understand more about the nature of suffering, the stigma, marginalisation, and isolation that mentally ill people endure, and how in a non-threatening environment, offering relationships of decency and respect, we are able to begin the process of healing some of that pain. Which, of course, connects with what we do here— because death, the dying process, can isolate people.

'We're frightened of death. We don't know how to deal with it and the suffering that goes with it. So there is value in offering patients and families a place where they can be real, and we can meet them in an authentic way, be with them and offer the support and care they need. And there's mutuality in this. It's not a one-way street, but rather a community where each of us is both giving and receiving. We really do receive so much, and it can be transforming for all of us.'

It is impossible to say for certain that Adrian Rhys-Mendoza deliberately adopted Viktor Frankl's uncompromising attitude towards his own fate. His upbeat, optimistic attitude could simply have been a lifelong habit. However, his attitude reflects Frankl's directive that, if suffering is inevitable, the task is to find out what life expects from us and to go for it, putting aside all our own expectations.

As an intelligent, caring person who was deeply concerned about the effects of his death on his family, Adrian gave a great deal of thought about how he would handle his own demise; what attitude he would adopt towards it, and how he would act it out. He was ill and weakened for months before his death. Unless he had made some sense out of his suffering and invested it with meaning, he couldn't have kept up such a consistently cheerful front. His family told me he was specific about his funeral instructions, and that in his detailed Will he took care of everyone. Making meticulous preparations, including those for your own funeral, is consistent with a workmanlike attitude towards a task to be done. In Adrian's case the task involved making a statement with his life.

Coming as he did from a large, warm and involved family, Adrian seemed intuitively aware of the impact his attitude towards death might have on his relatives. Perhaps he was aware that unresolved grief can go beyond a person's own life and be passed down as an invisible legacy from one generation to another, helping shape the spirit and expectations of a family group as surely as inherited genes help shape the body.

The subconscious plays an essential role in the healing process, so the dreams that Adrian's family had after his death were a natural phenomenon. However, as is commonly the case, they didn't leave the awakened dreamer suffused with a sense of pain and loss but with energy, delight and comfort.

These dreams speak not to any religion, but to having faith in faith.

Adrian felt that attitude—whether he infected his family and friends with grief or with optimism—really mattered. Independent of any organised religion he had found or created values that he respected. He made the decision to remain connected to his life and live it fully to the end. This course of action signified who he was. He had the satisfaction of leaving his family in grief but at peace. He loved life with a passion yet made it seem easy to let go and enter cheerfully into death. God only knows what it cost him. He died ten days short of his thirty-seventh birthday, a stack of travel brochures under his pillow.

# The Caregiver

*It is the secret sympathy,*
*The silver link, the silken tie,*
*Which heart to heart, and mind to mind,*
*In body and in soul can bind.*
　　—Sir Walter Scott, 'The Lay of the Last Minstrel'

In the past decade medical technology has developed to the point where many patients, who would previously have been confined to a hospital for their last weeks or months, are now able to die at home. Sophisticated catheters, syringe drivers, home oxygen dispensers, and other instruments make it possible for a professionally untrained carer, with back-up from a nurse or doctor, to provide terminal care at home. This technical development has coincided with a heightened social awareness about the way in which we live. There is nostalgia in the air, a looking back some sixty-odd years with the belief that life then was somehow simpler, purer, more natural, closer to the core of human nature.

Dying at home is one of the features of this roseate dream. Elisabeth Kubler-Ross and her many writings on death and dying have sensitised us to the potential grotesqueries of a hospital death: tubes sticking out of wasted bodies like needles on a porcupine, ventilators pushing lungs in and out, needles taped to swollen hands, and arc lights blinding sight as a team of shouting strangers attempt to pull the patient back from the brink. These senseless ends are still commonplace in most western hospitals. However, such 'heroic measures' apply mainly to crisis situations such as heart attacks and industrial and motor accidents. More insidious are the routine surgical interventions, drug fiddling and experimentation, intubations and skin-burning radiations inflicted on often ill-informed patients who are beyond any hope of respite or recovery.

A determination to avoid such an end—while benefiting from small, manageable medical technology such as syringe drivers or oxygen dispensers that ensure a degree of comfort—has been a major force in the development of palliative care. As palliative care increases, there is a parallel movement to return death and dying to the home wherever possible. Home is seen as offering privacy, comfort, familiarity, and the presence of treasured mementos of one's life. Home care is also good for hospital budgets in particular and society in general: viewing death is a healthy infusion of reality into a society that lives mainly in illusion.

In talking with family members who cared for a terminally ill patient at home prior to their entering McCulloch House, I was struck by the gap that exists between the benign images of home care and the realities. When the prime responsibility for care is centred on one person—as compared to the diffusion of responsibility in a palliative-care centre or hospital—the physical energy and psychological strength that are required are enormous. The primary caregiver, whether a member of the family or a health professional, not only brings their own psychological history into the situation—such as a prior death at home—but he or she can become the focus, a sort of depository, for the emotions of others involved. The setting of a public place such as a hospital helps tone down the likelihood of family in-fighting, but the privacy of the home can often furnish the opportunity for such negative fallout. Conversely home care often allows for the full expression of love.

Despite a lingering tendency to perceive dying at home as a traditional, cultural norm reflective of good family values, it is a custom that has been set aside in recent times. In fact, in the sixty years that have elapsed since dying at home was the usual practice, society has undergone such major changes that dying in a hospital has now become the norm. High divorce rates, women working, men raising children, family members located far apart, greater longevity and a paucity of nursing help are realities that aren't going to change. If we return to dying at home, who will do the caring? Will there be enough caregivers with enough income to survive without working, enough health, enough strength to lift and support the patient, enough freedom from other family duties, enough *virtue*—patience and compassion—to be the primary caregiver of a terminally ill person whose deterioration might stretch over days, week or months? Do our daily lives sufficiently mirror the lives of half a century ago to assume that home caregiving now can be the same as caregiving then?

These are the practical questions, but there are also ethical and psychological issues to ponder. What are the responsibilities adult children have to aged parents? What are the limits to sacrifices a working man or woman should ethically and legally be expected to make to care for a terminally ill loved one at home? Should an eighty-four-year-old man be expected to care for his eighty-two-year-old terminally ill wife? Do people want their living rooms turned into clinics? Does the surviving spouse find the bedroom the same comforting space now that their partner has died there? The answers to these questions will feed into the ultimate attitude society adopts towards the development of adequate palliative-care centres, and/or legalisation of euthanasia, because they relate directly to the basic question: *who is going to take care of whom in the years ahead and how will it be done?*

It is generally assumed that if one loves a dying person sufficiently and their care can be technically managed, dying at home is the ideal situation. This assumption is often infused with a high moral tone, making it difficult for a person to refuse responsibility for a relative's care. The fact is that many, probably most, people want to take care of their loved ones at home, but the assumption that they *should* loads their decision with potential guilt and works to preclude a choice based on the good of everyone in the family, including the patient. Apart from all the stress and complexities of today's family life, a factor that has been inadequately considered is the huge gap that exists between the nursing experiences of an ordinary lay person and the knowledge, wisdom and sense of familiarity that trained health professionals have from daily dealings with sickness and death over many years. This gap can make an ordinary person feel that such a responsibility is beyond his or her capacity.

Deep satisfaction and profound peace in having cared for a terminally ill loved one is frequently experienced by caregivers, but caregiving can also produce physical exhaustion, marital stress, despair, fear and resentment. Furthermore, it can disrupt other members of the family who are also entitled to consideration. In such cases, when death occurs, the carer feels overwhelming relief rather than grief. This sort of reaction can produce guilt and confusion, with a prolonged period of bereavement that may require counselling or some form of psychiatric intervention.

Health professionals, particularly palliative-care specialists, are well aware of the difficulties or even undesirable aspects of home care in some instances. But they, too, work under time and budget restrictions and are influenced by current pressures. Simply put, before society decides what is 'right' and develops any public policy influenced by an increased interest in dying at home, we should ask those who have been primary caregivers, and those who have been treated at home, what their experiences were and what they have learned from them. Both the carer and the patient are part of a society that has hidden sickness and death. And, like everyone else, they are subject to the same fears and ignorance that now surround these states. If public policy develops in the direction of home care for all terminally ill patients except for the most difficult cases, a necessary initial step should be a major public airing of the psychological states that can surround such a stressful event. Many people who appear highly suitable as the primary caregiver may have emotions that have never been dealt with properly, emotions they are ashamed to face.

Phillip is a nurse who was raised in Victoria and trained at the Mercy Hospital. He did geriatric nursing for a while, then finished a four-year course at Fairfield Infectious Diseases Hospital. He was recruited by an American company and worked for four years at Sherman Oaks, outside Los Angeles, and then on to the Visiting Nurses Association in Santa Barbara. Caring and thoughtful by nature, Phillip is the oldest of five children and describes his childhood as unhappy.

'When I was at school I thought I wanted to be a teacher,'

he tells me as we drink our coffee in the busy ground-floor cafeteria of Monash Medical Centre. After leaving school, though, he didn't know what he wanted. He worked for a year in an office, travelled around Australia, and was then out of work and restless. 'My childhood had been unhappy. Dad was one of ten brothers, all were known footballers in the district. I was overweight and felt inadequate. I didn't fit in. I was very sensitive and aware of others' emotions and, with time, I realised I was gay. This experience of not fitting in when I was young has taught me compassion and helped me with my work.'

Phillip says he entered nursing 'frightened and fearful of giving injections' but found he loved helping others and caring for the sick. The gentleness, which had caused him so much grief in his childhood, was now a valuable attribute.

'The years in California were both good and bad. At Sherman Oaks I spent four years working in an AIDS unit where there were about three to five deaths a week. Then I went to Santa Barbara. In some other ways I felt more effective there than here because nurses have much more authority. I was working in the Visiting Nurses Association's program, Hospice in the Home Care. Home care is more advanced in the United States because it's cheaper than hospitalisation. Doctors can certify a home as part of a Certified Hospice Association and give it standing orders, so that if a visiting nurse sees that more morphine is needed and the patient can stand it, he or she can call the pharmacy and have it delivered immediately. This streamlines the process and results in a very quick medical response.'

In Phillip's experience there is 'a significant difference' between a cancer death and an AIDS death. 'People terminally ill with cancer are so open to you, as if the cancer has opened up their lives. With AIDS there is a sense of a different openness, a sense of being able to say, "Yes, I am terminally ill and I am also gay." There is a sense of great relief that now you can be who you really are.'

'Euthanasia?' he repeats in response to my query. 'I've mixed feelings about it, but I have assisted in it in the United States. I'm open to it. But I wish what we were doing here at McCulloch House was available everywhere. The great majority of people are free of agitation or agonising death. They just need to be cared for properly when they're dying, as it's done here. Then the other question, euthanasia, hardly ever comes up.'


I discussed home care with fifteen relatives of McCulloch House patients, ten of whom had been caregivers, and ten patients who had experienced hospital care, home care, and care at McCulloch House. The interviews with the ten terminally ill patients were awkward in that I didn't feel it appropriate to broach the subject of their death directly. Instead I asked one broad, casually phrased question of patients: 'Do you feel more relaxed being at home or more relaxed being here?' And I made one flat statement in the hope of eliciting a reaction: 'It must have been difficult to leave your home.' I asked no questions of the caregivers, but simply let them describe their experiences. The following stories were selected because they reflect some common elements that emerged in each interview.

Karen Opolski is an attractive law clerk whose father, Dave, sixty-three, died of lung cancer. Karen and I meet in the McCulloch House lounge during her lunch break and, although pressed for time, she appears calm and unruffled.

'When Dad learned that he had lung cancer,' she says, 'his first reaction was, "I'll go to the Northern Territory [for euthanasia]." I would have helped him, gone with him. I would have done anything he asked me to.'

'Anything? Even kill him?' I ask.

'Anything,' she replies decisively. 'But it all happened so quickly, four months from diagnosis to death. He'd smoked but had given it up five years ago. My sister, Christine, and my partner, Glen, we wanted him at home to take care of him. We adored Dad. He was a man who made you feel safe, secure, loved. He came here from Yugoslavia after the war and became the foreman in a furniture construction plant. He had his hand out giving to others all the time. He was generous to a fault.

'He went so quick. But it wasn't quick enough. I believe absolutely in euthanasia. We wanted him at home. He wasn't frightened of death at all. He was a realist. At home we went through an extreme period of hope, with a diet of fresh vegetables, fruits, walks everywhere, lots of vitamins. And we surrounded him with love. Christine, Glen and I took his care in shifts. He was doing quite well, but then he got to the stage when we couldn't get fluids into him. He couldn't swallow. He lost the ability to move his arms and legs as the tumour spread to his spine and the nerves at the base of his skull. He needed drips and nasal-gastric tubes. We wanted to, but we couldn't sustain the care at home.

'My mother died at home at the age of thirty-nine. She had cervical cancer. She was a real advocate of a healthy lifestyle, no smoking, no drinking, lots of exercise. I was ten when she was diagnosed and my sister was eleven, so a lot was kept from us. We were twelve and thirteen when she died. She haemorrhaged. No one had prepared us for that. The only other person there with us was a family friend. We hadn't known it would be like that. Dad went to hell and back. It took him many years to get over her death. He didn't remarry. He did that for us. He devoted his life to caring for my sister and me. We would never have dreamed of not doing that for him.

'The treatment my mother had was the same as Dad had twenty years later. Radiotherapy with chemotherapy. Different drugs maybe, but the same effect. Things haven't changed much. We were lucky to get him into McCulloch House. Unless you've gone through it yourself, you don't know what it is. The last day was pretty horrid. He really struggled for breath, but he kept squeezing our hands. He was an atheist. He adored Mum. I mentioned her and tried to convince him she was waiting. We held him, rubbed him, kissed him. He loved his legs being massaged. He could feel the love and reciprocated as much as he could, despite his state.'

'What did you take away from these experiences?' I ask.

'I wanted him home to the end, but it was wonderful his being here at McCulloch House. The staff is so compassionate. They seem normal. I'm frightened of getting cancer. I don't know if I want any children. Who would take care of them if I died? I can't help thinking of that, the life cycle, how death's just part of it. It's made a difference in my attitude to strangers. I see everyone now not as young or old but as in a part of their life cycle. I went to a footy match recently and there were 80,000 people there all cheering, screaming and passionate, and I thought, Soon this will mean nothing to them.'


Judy Thomas is sixty-seven, a widow and a former school-teacher. She sits in her private hospital room propped up by cushions in a large armchair, a plaid Shetland wool shawl around her surprisingly plump shoulders and a blue blanket over her knees. Although she has ovarian cancer with extensive metastasis, has limited mobility and is within a few days of death, she is alert and has absolutely no pain. She seems unaware of the short time she has left.

'My daughter, Janet,' she begins, 'wants to take me home, but it's not my place, I sold that after my husband died and moved into an upstairs flat. I intended to travel a lot and wanted to simplify my life. I didn't want to be bothered with a garden any more. I never thought of getting sick. I've always been so healthy. If I could go back to my own home, that'd be good. But I don't want to go to my daughter's place. I've got no sentimental attachment, no particular feeling that I'm "home" when I'm there. I'm more relaxed here. I had two months at Janet's after my last surgery till the pain got so bad I had to come here. They have it under control now and say I can go back home. But I don't want to. I prefer it here. Maybe I'll get better enough here to go back to my own flat.

'Janet and her husband have a roomy place and she doesn't work, but I feel more at home here than I do there. I don't feel a nuisance here. I've heard them telling my grandsons—there are three of them, all teenagers—not to make any noise, to stop running, to turn down their radios. Noise bothers me, but I don't want my grandsons remembering me like an old granny that everyone had to creep around.

'There are other things, hygiene things, I prefer not to talk about, things I can't stand being involved in with my daughter. And then there's the door. She always leaves my door open so she can hear me. She means to make me feel secure by that, but I feel I've got less privacy there than I have here.

'I've always been independent. When my husband was alive, my independence would drive him mad. He died at home, in his sleep, of a heart attack. It was a shock, waking up and finding him gone, but sometimes I wish it had been me. I hope I'm not giving the impression my daughter's not good to me. She's wonderful. Lately I've felt quite short of breath. It's comforting here knowing there's nurses all around. I feel more secure than at home. In any case, I swore I'd never become a burden on my daughter as I've seen other women do.'

Peg Wright is a slight woman with a dazzling smile. She recently won the ten-kilometre Fun Run over-sixties category in Melbourne. She often brings a bunch of flowers for the McCulloch House lounge. Today she is carrying a mass of white and gold chrysanthemums. After she arranges them in a vase on the low coffee table, we sit and chat.

Peg cared for her husband, Ron, at home until a few days before his death from colon cancer, which had metastasised to his lungs and back. She was helped by their married daughter, Alice Carey. Peg was sixty-eight, Ron seventy-six, when he died.

'We'd been married forty-six years,' she says. 'We met after the war in Leggett's Ballroom in Prahran. In those days you didn't go out singly. You went out with girlfriends. You sort of went in a group and you eyed someone you liked and they sort of eyed you, and gradually after a few weeks or months you went out with them. I was twenty-one when we were married and he was twenty-nine. He was a bus driver, then he drove a truck for Myer's, and finally a taxi.

'After we found out he had prostate cancer, he had a year of very mild chemotherapy. He managed to win a couple of bowls championships after that, but then a two-year check-up revealed lesions in his lungs. I didn't like him being in hospital. I wanted to care for him. He wasn't a part of my life. He *was* my life. I wanted to do everything for him.

'Every night we'd sit down for a sherry together. One night he took down the Marmite jar and tried to drink out of that. His driving became erratic and he developed nervous mannerisms he'd never had before. He'd touch his face and head all the time, lightly with his fingers, but it was all the time. I'm not complaining, but the stress… He became obsessive, erratic. We found he had a brain tumour. At that point I began to wonder if we should do anything. The doctor told us the tumour was operable. I said to Ron, "It's your body, I'll back up any decision you make, whatever it is."

'After the operation, Ron became an angry man. The operation completely changed his behaviour. He had terrible tantrums. It was very hard after all our wonderful years together. The outbursts settled down after a while but flashes of them remained. He kept getting pneumonia. The last time it happened I called the ambulance and they took him to Jessie McPherson Private Hospital [attached to Monash Medical Centre]. I followed in our car. The waiting room was freezing. Ron was so terribly ill, so nauseated, but there were no beds. We had to sit there freezing, waiting. I couldn't help remembering all that he had been through in his life. He was in the landing at Balikpapan [Indonesia], with the artillery of the Seventh Division. It didn't seem right for him to have to sit there, or anyone to have to sit there, so nauseated and ill, and just frozen. Finally they got him onto a trolley, but he still had to stay in emergency.

'Ron had said to me years before he got sick, "If I'm ever in an accident, don't resuscitate me." I thought of that, and I made the hardest decision I'd ever made, but it was the biggest act of love. I said to the doctor, "Please don't try and do anything. He's had enough." So they got him into McCulloch House. I wanted to care for him at home. The tantrums had been hard and he didn't know us most of the time. I felt he wanted to go. I think letting him go into McCulloch House was my way of facing the fact I had to say goodbye. It was my final act of love. He only lasted a few days after that.'


A seventy-two-year-old retired accountant, John West is a tall, still-handsome man who was married to Joan for forty years. Three months earlier she had died at home of metastasised breast cancer. One of their two sons lives in London, another in Perth. As their mother's health declined, the son in Perth visited every three months, but the son in England came only for the funeral. John was supported by a palliative-care nurse who visited three times weekly. After John developed shingles, the nurse came once every day.

The family home in East Malvern—a bluestone Federation classic with a return verandah and wrought-iron lacework—speaks of a comfortable, conventional life. We walk through the centre hall to the back and settle into brightly coloured rattan chairs in a newly added solarium.

'These have been prosperous years in Melbourne and I had my own business,' John tells me. 'So I worked on, didn't retire until seventy, and as soon as I did Joan became ill. We were going to take a long holiday in England this year to visit our son and his family. Then Joan found a lump, and after that, well, our lives and everything else changed.

'That very day, as soon as we got the diagnosis, I made up my mind I'd look after her. I felt it was my duty, a duty that came with my marriage. Joan had been an excellent wife, a good mother and housekeeper. She had always supported me. Now it was my turn.

'The cancer was already in the lymph nodes, and Joan had

lost several friends who'd gone through everything—surgery, chemotherapy, hope, despair. We disagreed strongly on this issue. It was a stressful time. She refused to fight it, whereas I believed she should. I hadn't known her to be so stubborn. She lived only six months but, on the whole, it was quality time. Perhaps she was right.

'Joan died at home. I wasn't afraid of death, although I was afraid she might die while I wasn't there. When I left the room, I always hurried back. The nurse told me what to look out for—sweats, rapid breathing, confusion, maybe fading sight—but the only thing Joan had was that her breathing changed and she was delirious. I called the nurse, who came right away. Twice before Joan's breathing had changed and the nurse had always come. But this time it was the real thing. Joan just fell asleep. I was sitting beside her as if I were in the bed holding her in my arms. The nurse told me to keep on talking, that she could hear everything I was saying.

'I fall asleep every night in the bed that she died in. I feel very close to her. It gives me great comfort. I'd like to join her soon. People say I'll feel differently one day. I think they should keep their opinions to themselves.

'I couldn't have gotten through it without the palliative-care team. One day when the nurse was here I went out for a few groceries and drove into the back of another car. Nothing serious, but I've never had an accident before and it shook me up. The nurse pointed out how stressed I was and suggested I use a taxi for a while, that I had too much on my mind. What she said was obvious, but having someone else say it helped me. The telephone was another real problem. I didn't want to cut it off, but it would ring at the most inconvenient times. The nurse suggested I get an answering machine. That was another obvious thing, but I hadn't thought of it.

'The next-door neighbours helped a lot with mainly moral support. That's what I needed. Joan's breast—it was the left one—had an open wound, ulcerated with a very bad odour. Even with the windows open it was noticeable. That was the one thing I had to fight to overcome—the smell. I knew how hard it was for Joan. She'd always been a fussy woman. You'd say dainty. I changed the dressing twice a day. It was hard to look at it, but I did it for Joan. My next-door neighbours often popped in with a hot meal. Not once did they give the slightest indication of distaste, although the smell was pervasive. They're a young couple in their thirties. They were very friendly with Joan, who was a keen gardener. She'd helped them landscape their place and put in a garden of native plants and shrubs. I feel really grateful for their moral support and help.

'I'm going to stay with my son in Perth next week. He says I should go on to England. I'm not sure about that. I don't feel my boys really understood about their mother and me. My neighbours did, but they didn't. Ironic, isn't it? They kept trying to get me to put her into a hospital. They said caring for her was too hard on me. I wanted that responsibility, but they just didn't seem to hear me. I needed their reassurance, not resistance. Joan's mother died in hospital and Joan was terrified of that. It was stressful, but we were both more relaxed than if Joan had been in hospital. Joan never spoke directly about dying. There was no need. Towards the end she told me what she'd like by way of a service.

'I didn't expect my sons to be here, but I did expect them to support what I was doing. I needed that because I often felt isolated, cut off, despite the palliative-care team. The nurse knows my sons wanted me to put Joan in hospital, because they'd often phone and say the same thing to her. She says I should discuss it with them. Maybe I will. Their lack of understanding was disappointing, but I feel deeply satisfied that I did all I could.'


Alice Reid, fifty-nine, left work as a sales assistant to care for her chemist husband, Tim, who was suffering from brain cancer. Their three adult children lived interstate but visited frequently. Alice prefers to meet me in a neutral setting, so we get together at a small Italian restaurant in a side lane at the top of Collins Street.

'It was both my fault and not my fault that caring for Tim became so difficult,' she insists. 'Tim was actually easy to care for. He became immobile and incontinent a few weeks before he died, but the palliative-care team taught me how to use the special sheets and panties, so I managed quite well. The only surprise was how much laundry there was. It was endless.

'At times Tim didn't know any of us, and he'd act a bit belligerently. At other times he was clear-headed but very quiet. I could never tell from day to day what he'd be like. I'd wake up in the morning and think: just get through today. My children came as often as they could and that was a big help, because I didn't feel guilty taking time off if they were here. Toward the end my daughter took the sheets home nightly and delivered them the next day. When he got really sick, I couldn't keep up with the laundry.

'The problem was my two sisters-in-law. They never felt I was good enough for Tim. None of the Reid family did. He was the family prize. I left school at fifteen and went straight to work at Woolworths. We met by accident, at the beach, and took to each other right away. I was eighteen and he was twenty-one. He took me home. His father sat at the head of the table and scarcely spoke to me. When his mother was alone with me, she told me about other girls Tim knew, how well they dressed and how refined and polished they were. I'm mentioning this because all that hurt has come back since Tim died.

'For Tim's sake I've always tried to get on with his two sisters, Betty and Hester. Neither married. He was the man in their life. They were always phoning him and asking, "Could you just pop over for this? Could you just fix that for us?" He did their income tax and advised them in their financial affairs. They liked involving him. It kept them all knitted together, as if he were still their young brother. Sometimes I resented it, so did Tim, but we decided to just accept it.

'I went back to work part time in a shop ten years ago after the children left home. You should have heard Betty and Hester going on about my working in a shop, as if it was their business! I quit when Tim got sick. I made up my mind he wasn't going to die in hospital if I could help it. I should have seen what would happen. Betty and Hester started coming in every day. I had so many other people in and out—the palliative-care nurse, the physiotherapist, occasionally the doctor, my children, people to fix up the bathroom and make it safe and, of course, Tim's friends. I could control his friends, and even our children, by asking them to come at specific times. Betty and Hester never phoned to see if it was convenient. They just arrived. They always welcomed a cup of tea, but never got it themselves. They acted like guests, sitting down and waiting. My daughter, Sally, could see what was happening and told me I had to limit their visits. For Tim's sake I couldn't do that.

'They'd say, "This isn't a criticism, dear, just a comment," then they'd ask if I was sure, absolutely sure, Tim was getting the right medication or enough medication. On another day they'd suggest he appeared to be getting too much medication. They'd say to Tim, "Oh, you poor darling, your pillows need fluffing up," as if I wasn't doing my job right. I needed support, but they robbed me of my confidence. I began thinking that maybe he'd be better off in a hospital. Sometimes they'd arrive when Tim was lucid, and then they'd hint I'd exaggerated when I said he was confused. This infuriated me. And it really hurt. I followed exactly what the nutritionist suggested by way of food, but they'd suggest something different. "At least just try it," they'd say. I'd reply that he couldn't swallow or digest it properly and then they'd act as if they hadn't heard me.

'There was another thing that drove me up the wall. Sometimes when Tim's male friends would come they'd have the cheek to act like the hostess. Then they'd offer tea and even make it, as if it were their home, not mine. At other times if they didn't like one of his visitors, they'd hover around Tim until the visitor left.

'There were times when I felt the three of us were silently fighting over Tim's body. Who would get control and possession of it? The showdown came one day when I was so done in I was beginning to wonder if and when it would all end. Tim had been hallucinating during the night, and I'd found it so distressing that I got the palliative-care nurse to come over. Finally Tim fell into a deep sleep at about eight in the morning. I took a bath, took the phone off the hook, and settled down for a sleep in his room. About an hour later Hester and Betty arrived.

'Later that day I heard the two of them chattering away to him about their income tax, as if he were well and rational! When I went in, I saw this look on his face, a terrible fear. He was hearing all this familiar stuff, but he couldn't follow a word of it. He looked lost and terrified. I could have killed them. I shoved them out of the bedroom and told them to leave. Then I sat down and thought about what I'd done. After an hour I phoned them and said from then on they had to call before they came. When Betty said I sounded 'rather peculiar' and suggested I was having a nervous breakdown, I hung up. I had never hung up on anyone before in my life.

'Tim died the following night in his sleep. I phoned our children and Betty and Hester at once, and everyone came over. It looked as if I would have a reconciliation with them, but now that Tim's gone I doubt they have any real interest in coming here. I'm just as happy. Sally has told me to get them out of my life. They weren't being malicious, just their usual thoughtless selves, but that can have the same effect. I should have had the nerve to take control earlier, but I didn't for Tim's sake. If Tim had been in a palliative-care centre, maybe I could have had the staff help me with controlling the times of his sisters' visits. I might have gone to the social worker and gotten help as to how to handle them. I wouldn't have let them create all that tension and rob me of my peace. I think Tim felt it. It should have been a special time for both of us, but those women turned it into a nightmare.'


Vicky Boyd is tucked up in bed in the front bedroom of a modest Dandenong home. The room is as dusky as twilight. The fresh floral curtains are drawn, and Vicky's slight form is barely outlined by the blue-patterned eiderdown. There are four of us—Vicky's mother, Dr Peter Martin, a nurse from the Dandenong palliative-care service and myself. Peter sits towards the head of the bed, close to Vicky. The nurse stands at the end, I sit by the side and the mother is by the door.

Vicky is married, is the mother of a seven-year-old and has advanced ovarian cancer. Recently she has been given a syringe driver which is butterflied onto her arm. It delivers a specific dose of analgesics whenever she feels the need for it. A faint down of hair covers her bald head. She is twenty-seven and probably will not live more than two or three months. So far she has given no indication to anyone that she is aware of this. Vicky's mother confides that the previous evening Vicky and her husband had vigorously disagreed over her refusal to have any more chemotherapy.

'How are you feeling, Vicky?' Peter asks.

'Shithouse,' Vicky retorts.

'You're due for chemotherapy in two weeks, so there's a big decision to be made,' Peter says.

'Yeah, well, I've made it.'

'She knows what she wants,' Vicky's mother says brightly. There is a fixed, brave smile on her harried face. 'She wants a different kind of chemo, or no more chemo at all.'

'Look,' Vicky says, trying unsuccessfully to lift her head, 'it's me lying on the bed. I'm the one to decide. I told him [her husband] last night to piss off, and I meant it. What I want to know is why I feel so lousy. I'm tired all the time. When am I going to feel better?'

'Do you think more chemo would help, Vicky?' Peter asks.

'Well, the last lot didn't, did it? All I want to do is get up and maybe make tea. Get tea for my husband. No big deal. Why can't I do it?'

Obviously she deeply misses the ordinary traffic of daily life. The feistiness has drained from her voice. How much does she know and understand? How much does her mother know and understand?

'What do you think, Vicky?' Peter asks. He suspects she knows the truth and gently encourages her to acknowledge it. It is now nine months since her chemotherapy began and Vicky spends all day in bed.

'You're the doctor, aren't you?' she retorts. 'I'm just saying I don't want any more chemo. Anyone tells me to, no problem, I'll tell them to piss off.' She pauses. 'I've got a kid, you know. Seven. He's doing good at school. I want to make it to Christmas.'

'Of course you'll make it to Christmas,' her mother breaks in, guffawing loudly, trying to drag confidence into the room by sheer tone of voice, by moving briskly to jiggle the blinds, by straightening a doily on the chest of drawers. 'What are you talking about? You'll make it for Christmas, for ten more Christmases.'

Vicky ignores her mother and looks right at Peter. 'I like it here. I like it at home. Mum looks after me real good. I can see my husband, even if he does piss me off, nagging about having more chemo. I can see my kid before he goes to school and after school.'

Vicky knows. And she has let Peter know she knows, despite her mother's nervous denials. 'Keep me at home,' Vicky is saying. 'I don't want to go into a hospital. I want to face whatever is ahead right here.'

We leave the room while Peter examines Vicky. In the car he says to the nurse, 'The husband apparently knows the truth, but the mother needs to be helped to come to terms with it. She's still in denial. And Vicky must be put on opioids. She has very palpable masses. She nearly jumped off the bed when I barely touched her. And could you arrange for someone to talk to the boy? It may be very hard for him to understand what's going on. He's been kept out of the picture. The little chap should be prepared for what's going to happen.'


Gladys Cunningham, the mother of six adult children, lies stretched out in an upholstered reclining chair in the breakfast room of her Dandenong home. Nearby is a sunroom filled with potted plants. Outside, the manicured lawn, the glossy rockeries, the thick herbaceous borders speak of years of careful gardening. Gladys's hair is pitch-black, her body short and stocky, her manner open-hearted and blunt.

A year ago, at seventy, she was diagnosed with cancer. Until her condition deteriorated a few days before this visit, she managed with her own doctor and the help of a nurse. Her meeting with Peter today is her first with a palliative-care specialist.

Peter gets down to business. 'What's your understanding about your illness?'

Gladys cuts to the chase. 'I know I can't get any better. I've got it in the lungs, bones. I've got fractures of the spine, crushed vertebrae.'

'Did they say where the cancer is from, the site of the original tumour?' Peter asks.

'Ah, they don't know,' she replies, a tinge of disparagement in her voice. 'It took them over three months to even find it. Last year I was sick, lost weight, had every test under the sun, but nothing showed up. It wasn't a big shock. The doctor thought it was cancer, but they couldn't get onto it. I had radiotherapy three or four times. After the first lot, I felt great. But the pain came back, and I had it again. I used to go to Bali every year. I'm slow-moving now, but I've got no pain. None at all. So last month I took off for Bali.'

'Mum knows a lot of people there and everything went well,' Gladys's daughter, Jenny, adds. Later she confides that Gladys spent most of the time in her hotel room, too tired to go out.

'I was healthy till I was seventy,' Gladys muses. 'Funny, isn't it? No pills, no headaches, never even took aspirin. Nothing.

Still, I don't feel too bad. I did late Saturday night, though. I went to bingo and after I came home I had a wall of pain all around my waist and back. I didn't think I'd make it. I rang Jenny. It came on quick and went away. I slept all night, but it came back in the morning. I'm feeling all right now. I'm taking liquid morphine. I've got osteoporosis. Don't know if it's osteoporosis or cancer that's causing the pain.'

'Mum was always very independent,' Jenny says. She looks at her mother with tender amusement. 'She worked in a factory till she was sixty-five. She could chop down a tree without difficulty.'

'I took morphine tablets with me to Bali,' Gladys says. 'Now I'm taking it in liquid. I hope I don't become addicted to it.'

At this point her son, Rob, joins the conversation. 'No, Mum, I tell you. There's no problem if you're sick. You can be on it as long as you want to be on it if you're sick.' He turns to Peter. 'Mum's only been on it for a few days, and I keep having to give her my morphine-myth talk.'

'You've hit the nail on the head,' Peter says, a note of surprise in his voice. Few people are aware of morphine's unique, still mysterious characteristic: if the body is in pain there is no danger of addiction. Only if the body is healthy and well, and the drug is taken for psychological reasons, will addiction follow.

'I can't sleep in bed,' Gladys volunteers. 'I sleep in this chair.' She leans back and stretches her legs out. 'In bed I prop myself up but slide down. I can get off and walk from this chair.'

'How's your appetite?' Peter asks.

'Like a horse. And I like my lollies.'

Peter then broaches the subject of palliative care. 'It's offered to those with serious illnesses,' he explains. 'It's about worries and cancer. Some people lock it all up. If you want to blow off steam...'

'Ah, no,' Gladys says. 'I get a bit mad, but I don't hide it. Some people even hide their age, but that don't bother me. I think, ah, shit, I did want to go overseas this year, but I can't do it. I look at my mother's cousin, fit as a fiddle, ninety-three years old, lives in a big house by herself.'

'Well, sometimes you build up issues, start thinking of your family's welfare, things like that,' Peter explains. 'Palliative care is about information, too, so you can make choices. Your family might want different information from what you want.'

'I tell you I didn't like the specialist I had,' Gladys interjects. 'Paternal. I didn't like that. But my doctor now I like. He gives me a pat on the back.'

'We've all got different styles,' Peter comments blandly. 'Some run towards it, some run away, some stay in the middle. Dandenong palliative service has a pastoral-care worker— not religious—to let people blow off steam and listen. Things like losing your everyday independence. You can talk about it.'

At first Gladys seems not to have heard. 'I love my garden. I just sit and knit. I love my thirteen grandchildren. I've got a great-grandchild, too. Love my kids. Love my house. My son, Rob, is going to stay with me. Jenny lives around the corner. Never any need for me to go anywhere else.' She pauses, then says, 'Used to go to Bali twice a year for six weeks. Guess that's finished. No thanks. Your name's Martin, is it? I just want to stay here, get through it best I can, not looking on the dull side, not looking ahead. I can stay here till, you know…?'

'I don't see why not,' Peter says.

Gladys sighs. 'Ah, shit, that's the way to go.'

Maria is a registered nurse at McCulloch House. Married to an agricultural scientist, she is the mother of four young adults and is the deputy state commissioner of the Girls' Brigade, an international movement similar to Girl Guides but with a Christian orientation. Trained at Mooroopna, a base hospital near Shepparton, she worked in the surgery department of Dandenong and District Hospital for twelve years.

We have been attempting to meet for days, but Maria and her fellow staff members have been too busy dealing with the deaths of two patients and the arrival of three more. So we cancel our plans for lunch and sit at the large oak table in the McCulloch House lounge.

'From the time I was a little girl I wanted to be a nurse,' she says. 'My grandmother died in her fifties, but she was bedridden for years and my mother nursed her all that time. There were three girls in my family and we all became nurses.

'When I started working, I often felt patients were short-changed, that they needed skills other than nursing. I remember one night a surgeon dropped by a woman who had had some diagnostic tests. He simply said, "You have a mass in your stomach. We're going to take it out in two days' time." Then he turned on his heel and left. The way surgeons tell their patients is terrible sometimes. The older surgeons can't cope if the patient starts crying. I remember another patient—it was at night and nobody was around, no family or friend—and the doctor said, "We can't do anything for your leg. We're going to take it off, possibly below the knee, maybe above." And she was seventy.

'I find working in palliative care so rewarding because it's the alternative to the technical approach medicine takes these days. I've seen people dying in a general ward. There's often four in a bedroom, with a cloth screen, so everything said to or by the patient and family is heard. There's no privacy, no staying over. If a person stays over, they have to sit up all night in a chair. There are no recliners. There's no time to die slowly, peacefully, with all the beepers, the machines, the vacuum cleaners, the traffic. Everyone's busy, and it's a case of "Go ahead, die by yourself." Here we hold their hand, talk quietly to them. Most patients here are on a maintenance dose, and if that isn't working in three-quarters of an hour, we give it again, and then again. Any dose that we give isn't enough to kill a patient.

'The way GPs and the specialists look after their cancer patients is terrible sometimes. They're twenty years behind the times. They always think there is another operation they can do. A friend of mine had cancer in both liver and bone. This doctor wanted to do surgery, and I told her to ask him if she'd be able to walk and talk after it. Well, that was it. She didn't go for it but she had six good months.

'There are some surgeons who say, "Let's pull out and hand it on to palliative care. Let's give them quality of life, not quantity." Many Australian patients aren't prepared to ask for it, or to say to their doctor, "I don't want any more. I simply will not go for that surgery." Nor will they say, "I refuse to have chemo." They aren't aware of their rights and, if they are, they won't exercise them. They can pay for that in terms of suffering. I've taught our children to question everything.

'There is so much to be done to improve things. We've become so technical in medicine that there are huge areas of neglect. Some frail old people who are looking after their spouse or partner are told, "We'll send someone in to give the patient a shower." But what about the rest of the twenty-four hours?

'There's a critical need to address attitude towards decision-making at the end of life—culture, ethics, what a doctor's responsibilities are, what a nurse's responsibilities are, what the attitude should be towards pain control. Some doctors never look at their basic attitudes. They never think that what might be right for them might not be right for the patient. Because they would elect to have chemotherapy doesn't mean the patient would. We've got to attack the idea that what you're thinking is what the patient thinks.'

As the movement to care for the terminally ill within their own homes grows stronger, the need to air all issues surrounding dying at home becomes greater. The development of high-tech home care, and the provision of visiting palliative-care teams helps eradicate the boundaries between hospital and home. A living room or spare bedroom can be turned into a clinic, and an array of antibiotics, analgesics, home oxygen dispenser, hospital bed, commode and other such objects have the power to change the entire atmosphere of the home.

Most people want to die at home, if they have a home, and most people want to care for their loved ones at home, if they can. Having one room of the house, even the main room, turned into a clinic means nothing to some people as long as they can care for their loved one at home. Other people find that the trappings of a hospital in the private sphere of their home robs their home of the values they not only treasure but need to get through their own lives: a sense of home as a refuge, a stressless, private place of comforting and familiar rituals.

The decision to become a caregiver to a terminally ill person should be taken with the greatest freedom and not under the shadow of a false moral prescriptive that it is 'better'. It will only be 'better' for the patient and caregiver if some potential limitations are acknowledged at the beginning and, in certain cases, patients are counselled that home care is on a trial basis. The multiple range of situational factors such as employment, space, the presence of small children and physical strength will be evident to anyone involved in the decision-making process. But other critical factors such as physical exhaustion, an unacknowledged fear of death, loss of identity, a sense of isolation and unresolved family relationships can turn the best-meant effort into a situation heavy with resentment and guilt.

That is the worst scenario. The experiences of Karen Opolski, John West and Peg Wright showed how being the primary caregiver can give profound satisfaction. Although Karen and Peg both finally relinquished their father and husband respectively to McCulloch House, they had the immense pleasure of knowing they had given everything they had to give. Karen's comments regarding her mother's home death—'Nobody had prepared us for that [haemorrhage]'—reflects a history that could well have excused her and her sister, Christine, from caring for their father at home. Young and healthy, and aided by Karen's partner Glen, they were able to care for Dave in eight-hour shifts until the specifics of his deterioration demanded the technical relief that only a palliative-care centre could supply.

Peg Wright felt that her decision to put Ron into palliative care wasn't just acknowledging that his case had become unmanageable. She was also acknowledging and accepting that it was time for Ron to die, as well as honouring his earlier expressed wish not to be resuscitated. She knew that McCulloch House would give no resuscitation or treatment—that it would only provide comfort and control any pain.

John West was a reserved, old-fashioned man. He was

physically strong and had a well-equipped home. Furthermore, Joan's illness was manageable at home until her death. John didn't lack affection or respect, but it was his sense of duty, and an awareness of Joan's fear of dying in hospital, that led him to become the primary caregiver. Like everything else he did in life, he did the job carefully and well, and felt let down by his sons when they didn't appear to appreciate this.

Judy Thomas had a daughter and son-in-law willing to care for her full time but, after a lifetime in her own home, found the 'nuisance' aspects of being in someone else's home intolerable. Her reference to 'hygiene things' probably referred to the fact that, as a morphine taker, she suffered from constipation and needed her daughter's help in inserting rectal suppositories. She had a sense of greater privacy and independence in a palliative-care centre and felt comforted by being close to expert medical help with whom she had no personal relationship. She felt more capable of maintaining her strong sense of identity away from her daughter's home, a factor that counted since she didn't wish to leave her grandsons with memories of 'a granny you had to creep around'.

Alice Reid entered a situation that appeared straightforward but, because there was a long-standing problematic relationship with in-laws, what should have been an enriching time between husband and wife turned into a nightmare. Alice had not been aware that her tolerance of her sisters-in-law was made possible by the strength and love of Tim. When Tim became ill and dependent on her, that support vanished and Alice found herself incapable of defending her 'territory' against the claims of two strong women. The sisters-in-law, in turn, had never felt Alice to be a match for their brother, and this attitude surfaced powerfully in their professed concern for the quality of his care.

Alice allowed the pressure to build to an explosive point before having the courage to confront the situation. The manner in which she handled it caused her distress and profound resentment at precisely the time she needed to feel strong and at ease with herself. Alice took charge of her husband's care with skill and devotion, but the satisfaction that should have accompanied the successful conclusion of her work was marred by her inability to take charge of, and protect, her own 'territory'.

In the American book *Bringing the Hospital Home*, one of the basic questions asked is: who is suffering? In view of the state in which a terminally ill patient lives, this might seem a remarkably selfish question to ask. But asking and answering hard questions has become a necessity in the face of changing health-care demands and changing resources. An essay in this same book on the social and ethical implications of home care by John D. Arras and Nancy Neveloff-Dubler states:

> 'Most decisions about care in the home concern the issue of how to live, not whether to live, and these decisions usually implicate the real and weighty interests of persons other than the patient, persons whose lives, careers, and emotional balance may be drastically upset by a decision to participate in a home-care plan... The systematic exclusion of the interests of family and friends who provide care at home is untenable and unjust. Others besides the patient have legitimate needs and the resulting conflict should not always be resolved in favour of the patient.'*

---

* John D. Arras & Nancy Neveloff-Dubler, 'Ethical and Social Implications' in *Bringing the Hospital Home: Ethical and Social Implications of High-Tech Home Care*, (ed.) J. D. Arras.

In the past it has usually been women who have nursed the sick and terminally ill. Traditionally all women have been defined by their capacity and ability to care, and the basic assumption underlying this—that caregiving is the natural domain of women—is still prevalent today. But is it related to today's realities?

Nel Noddings, another contributor to *Bringing the Hospital Home*, comments:

> 'Traditionally, the only acceptable excuse a woman has been able to offer is competing duties to care... Because it was thought that women *want* to care, any woman who resisted the caregiving role was thought to be "unnatural". Another aspect of this tradition is equally pernicious. Because it was thought that any woman could provide nursing or child care, all those tasks associated with direct bodily care have been devalued... It is often thought that a female homemaker should contribute her own labour because she is not a wage earner, and even women who earn a small wage outside the home are expected to give up their unprofitable work to provide direct care. A man in the latter situation would rarely experience such an expectation.'

*Bringing the Hospital Home* provides an American perspective on home care, but the questions raised are equally valid issues in Australia. Many Australian women are sandwiched, happily or otherwise, between caring for their young children and their elderly parents. Other women, who are caring for elderly parents, are elderly themselves. Because of the weight of stereotypical roles they have no choice.

The developing health-care crisis will increasingly look to high-tech home care as part of the palliative-care system. The quality of the care given and received will depend on who the caregiver is, their physical strength and stamina, their emotional stability and secondary supports, their general competency and, finally, the true nature of their relationship with the terminally ill person. If the objective is to make death simply a part of life, a part in which the terminally ill can live fully until death, then these issues must be honestly aired and taken into full account.

# Faith

*That he who many a year with toil of breath*
*Found death in life, may here find life in death.*
  —Samuel Taylor Coleridge, 'Epitaph for Himself'

I t is early June 1997 and I have been at McCulloch House for six weeks. I have also visited other palliative-care units and a couple of nursing homes. And with Dr Peter Martin I was able to see palliative-care patients in their own homes. My initial need to be in the middle of the suffering and dying, problems and solutions, is as intense as ever. My reasoning is that if I don't select my cases, if I make the realities explicit, don't sift out but allow everything in, I will find the answer to my original question: *Is euthanasia desirable or necessary, or could accessible palliative care supplant the need for it?*

But that isn't happening. Some days I wake up with an unequivocal conviction: God gave us intelligence and compassion and we're supposed to exercise them both. For God's sake, let's have the faith to exercise compassion for those who ask for it and end their suffering. Then I go to bed and furiously ask:

How can we say that euthanasia is all right in a culture that is so expedient, so greedy? How can it be 'safe' and limited when government after government slashes the health-care budget? Who would be the prime targets for emptying hospital beds?

A few days later I wake up and think: Euthanasia is practised by a few doctors now in our acute-care hospitals. It's total hypocrisy to pretend it doesn't go on. Wouldn't legislation that tightly controlled and monitored it be preferable to all this two-faced cant where nobody knows what the hell is going on and everyone pretends nothing is going on? Before going to bed that night I say to myself: For the state to sanction euthanasia is just another step in the wrong direction for society to take. Did making abortion legal honour life more? Will making euthanasia legal honour life more? Or will it, like abortion, become a commonplace way of life?

I am aware, as I agonise on my mental seesaw, that among people who know by experience what pain can do I have a lot of company. None question the creativity and power of palliative care to provide the best possible life until the end, as well as the best possible death. All recognise that palliative care isn't a panacea for all the ills of dying. Those who know pain's power recognise the redemptive potential of palliative care, as well as its limits, and such knowledge can work against the unshakable confidence of those either for or against euthanasia.

When I realise how much company I have in my indecisiveness, I think of other possibilities—that I will never make up my mind, that I will never find an answer, that this struggle will go on forever. Or maybe I will learn what the right answer is on my own deathbed, when it is too late to do anything, too late to ask for mercy killing or too late to stop the doctor who approaches with a potassium-loaded needle, too late to follow

Emile Zola's dictum that I so love: 'to live life out loud'.

One thing I have learned is that common sense has no part to play in providing any answer. Common sense can't account for the audacious response so many patients feel they have to make towards the chaos in which they find themselves. If common sense ruled, they would all have killed themselves. What can I hope to find that will swing the vacillating tide and throw me onto a rock of certitude? Why, for instance, did Antonio 'Tony' Dimattina choose to go on living when tumours the size of grapefruit stuck out of his rectum? He had no fear of death. Was it the will to live? Or was it the possession of something solid and permanent, some internal quality with the toughness of steel and the allure of gold?

Tony's life was not unlike that of many immigrants who came to Australia in the late 1940s and early 1950s. He was born near Foggia, Italy. His father was a poor fisherman and Tony started full-time work at the age of eight. When Tony was a tall, strapping youth of seventeen, he met twelve-year-old Angelina, who lived a few streets away. Tony was determined to have a better life than his father had had. He completed high school at night and went to Switzerland, where factory workers were scarce and pay was high. When Angelina turned seventeen they became engaged, and four years later they married. Soon after, they returned to Switzerland where their daughter, Rosina, was born. When Rosina was six, joining a vast migration winding down from Europe, they moved to Australia.

They loved Australia from the moment they arrived, thinking that it was a land of extraordinary largesse and liberation. In fact, in the thirty years that followed they never knew a moment of homesickness or regret. At first they lived with some strangers, an Italian family whose matriarch treated Tony and Angelina as her son and daughter.

Rosina, who could speak no English, first attended Oakleigh primary and went on to Sacred Heart Girls' College five years later after the Dimattinas bought a house in Huntingdale. In her early teens Rosina developed problems with her left eye. Several operations by a Collins Street specialist couldn't rectify the problem, and at seventeen Rosina lost the sight in her left eye. At nineteen trouble developed in her right eye. The specialist identified the problem as a dropped retina, the cause of her earlier loss of sight. The family flew to Rome, but four surgeries failed to help. At nineteen Rosina was blind.

'My father got sick when I lost my sight,' Rosina says now. Her voice is warm and clear, but her attitude is marked by sorrow. She sits opposite me at her kitchen table, her eyes closed and her head slightly down. Nearby, in the beautifully tiled kitchen, Rosina's mother makes coffee, pausing from time to time to tell her story.

'I believe that's when his sickness started,' Rosina continues. 'Instead of talking about my loss of sight he held it inside. The subject made him very sad and depressed. I felt I had to do something with my life, so I did a life training course at the Blind Institute. We all cried that day. We weren't expected to be like that. I learned to do cooking and shopping, and there I met my husband, Mark. I was very lonely. Most people don't want to put up with blind people. I thought, no point in staying alone. I want company, a relationship. My husband is partially blind. Mark and I now have two beautiful children, a daughter, Pia, and a son, Peter. But that's when Dad got sick—when I became blind.'

Angelina, a small slight figure in black, stands by the table and picks up the story. 'My husband never sick. One night my brother-in-law ring to say my mother die in Italy, aged ninety, and Tony get very upset. He go to bathroom and call me to come see. Lots of blood, lots. We go to GP in morning and he send us to specialist at Moorabbin. Tony have a colonoscopy, and when the sister call me to pick him up, she say, "You need to see the doctor. Your husband has big sickness." My husband say to me, "Why you crying? Much better to see truth." But when doctor say, "You have cancer of bowel," Tony was shocked. "What you saying?" he ask. The doctor say again, "You have a cancerous growth." But Tony ask again, shocked, "What you saying?"

Angelina wrinkles her clear, unlined face and holds out her hands as if carrying a weight. 'The tumour in his bowel was gross. He have an operation and they put bag in. Very sick, but all the time smiling. After three or four months, he get better, get used to bag, and encourage other people who have bag.' The surgery Angelina refers to, a colostomy, involves making an artificial opening from the colon or large intestine. A disposable bag is attached to the opening so that the patient's faeces are eliminated there and not through the rectum.

'Then after three years, in 1992,' Rosina continues, 'Dad started getting pain, rectal pain, very bad. The doctor decided there was no cancer. Then eight months of terrible pain, X-rays, tests, and always the doctor says, "No cancer."'

Angelina interrupts. 'So finally I say I want to see another doctor. My husband can't sleep because of pain. And we go to another doctor, who say, "Your husband has cancer again." Poor Tony! He fall asleep standing up. I make special cushion for him. He can't bear his bottom to sit on chair.'

'So he went into therapy every day for six weeks,' Rosina adds. 'Mum took care of him every day. He had terrible burns. All the skin was cracked, very red, right down the middle of his bottom. They stopped after six weeks and then he couldn't urinate. Another operation and he couldn't walk. They put a hole in his belly button to pull the wee out. The doctor said he now had cancer in the groin. Dad accepted it. He said, "I've got one bag on one side and now another on the other." He didn't say, "I'm not going to do it." He stayed cheerful, even when the wee-wee bag would slip off and he'd get wet.'

At this point Angelina weeps, then says, 'I give him too much encouragement.' She pours coffee while tears scald her face. 'He say to me, "Angelina, I can't understand it. My daughter is blind, I am sick, but I'm a good worker." I think, maybe God want him. He couldn't drive, couldn't sit, couldn't sleep. He try to sleep leaning against the wall, like this.' Angelina closes her eyes and, standing against the wall, feigns sleep.

'Cancer now in his lungs,' she continues. 'He is on liquid morphine for four years. After second operation, he have too much morphine and he get infection in blood for two months. But all the time nice, never angry. "God will help us," he say. Nurses say to me, "Your husband go to paradise."'

Now Angelina's voice, sweet and sad, becomes infused with bitterness. 'If this happen to me, I want nothing. I no do this. You suffer too much. We strong Catholics, but I no do this. My husband say, "God help me. Make my pain better." He never lost the faith.'

Tony Dimattina was the first patient at McCulloch House in February 1996 and came in for respite treatment nine times before he died. 'Most of my life going back and forth,' Angelina says. 'I told Dr Jackson [Kate Jackson, a staff specialist], "I want my husband home. You do this for me." Dr Jackson say, "We do it for you." One month at McCulloch House, one month home.'

All the treatment at McCulloch House was palliative, none curative, but Tony held on. 'I don't want to die until you can see again,' he told Rosina. 'I want to be here to help you. You and the grandchildren need me.' Now in extreme discomfort, Tony finally lost the ability to eat or drink.

Michael Ashby and Peter Martin consulted with him. There was nothing they could do except, if he wished, put in a feeding tube. It could go down the gullet, or into his side and directly into the stomach. They explained that sometimes the liquid from the stomach came up into the lungs. Neither doctor wished to do either procedure. They wanted him pain-free and comfortable, but the whole objective of palliative care is to eliminate pain and let nature take its course. They clearly intimated this. On the other hand, the patient's autonomy and his or her right to choose or refuse treatment is paramount. Tony opted for a tube down his gullet, but after further discussion accepted the doctors' preference that it go in his side.

'Four days later,' Angelina tells me, 'on Moomba Day, he get up several times. He go into garden and walk around the corridors. I buy his gown in Italy, dark green with black lapels. I say to him, "You want a wash?" I always wash him.' She holds up her closed fist. 'Like this, the tumours on his rectum, big, hard, like rocks. You see them, sticking out the hole. My husband very sick but never stink. He say to me, "Angelina, I can't stay any more. I'm very tired. I feel like killing myself. I have to go. You look after Rosina, Pia, and Peter." When I say no, he say, "Look at my face. I am just bones." I say, "No, you still beautiful. When you come better, you look all right." At 4.30 a.m. the next night the phone ring. I drive to hospital. Next morning very peaceful, like an angel he died.'

'He died at eleven in the morning,' Rosina says. 'At 9.30 I said, "Wake up, Dad. Do you want a drink?" But his legs were already stiff. His whole body was getting stiff. Only his heart kept on beating. Dad made us strong, and now we don't know how to cope.'

I am sitting with the social worker, Barbara, in a quiet nook at the end of one of the modern wings of McCulloch House. Barbara is a mature woman with short red hair and a lot of quiet style. She hesitates, hunting for the truth, before responding to my question about what it is like to work in McCulloch House.

'This is a much more revealing situation than in ordinary counselling,' she says. 'In a hospital environment you connect very intimately with people. In a community agency, for instance, I wouldn't reveal anything about myself, but here you connect with people through a social exchange. I simply introduce myself to the patient and family as being here to support them emotionally, and if they need resources in the community such as legal help, I'll access that for them.

'One of the difficulties from my work viewpoint is that sometimes the stays are brief and it's hard to make connections. At times I think that we get too focused as to what happens with the family at this time. We tend to believe we're the only ones who finally connect with these people at the end of their lives and we don't allow for the fact that this is just a moment in time, although a very important moment. There may have been perhaps years of treatment and involvement with staff elsewhere.'

Barbara pauses, then adds, 'What is critically important is to get the balance, seeing this event as part of the whole from the time they were born. My view of life is longitudinal, a circle view of birth, life, death, rebirth, in which the role of McCulloch House staff is important but not the be-all and end-all. We support the families in whatever way we can, and then they move on to the next phase of their lives. I follow families for a while and then let go.'

People who do not have an encompassing view may go on

with life in a full way, she says, but their relationships and their physical health can suffer. 'I have seen a lot of people grieving for past losses and never come to terms with them. I don't say "resolve". I prefer "incorporate". Some people can resolve their losses, but most people come to incorporate this loss into their future living. Some people can incorporate terrible tragedies, others can't. There have been too many previous losses, such as a loss of one's native country or the failure of a parent to parent you. You see quite a few adult children by the bedside of a parent who has abused them, and there's a great deal of anger, followed by a lot of guilt.'

I am struck by Barbara's tone of easy authority and knowledge when she says how often she has witnessed the way in which one loss brings back the pain of previous losses. 'Nevertheless,' she says, 'if you are able to come to terms with a loss in a reasonable way, you can incorporate it.'

'I know that people go on after loss,' she continues. 'I have changed so much myself. My husband and I left South Africa with our three sons and came here in 1980. Three years later, without any prior warning, he dropped dead of a heart attack. He was forty. I was thirty-seven. I was a married woman. I didn't work. I'd never been to university. I was used to entertaining couples and going out to dinner with other couples. I didn't have one woman friend who was single. My husband's death threw me into a totally different life.

'I went to La Trobe Uni and did social work. I started to meet single women and go to movies and out to dinner with them. I enlarged my circle. I became a feminist. In our society we grow up in competition with other women, but when women get past a certain age they can get very close. I found an interesting world filled with friendship.'

Some years after her husband's death, her eldest son, aged

twenty-three, was killed in a car crash. 'Within eight years,' she tells me, 'I lost my husband, mother, father and son. The loss of my son impacted very heavily on us as a family. One person's grief impacts on another person. I have a very supportive partner and two surviving sons. Because I did it, because I survived, I know other people can, too. Once they have worked through the initial trauma, they get their lives together in a much more meaningful way, particularly in their relationships.

'I am really surprised at how much I can enjoy things, just pottering around the house, or playing some golf, or being with friends. All of this, all of life, is about living more fully. Working here helps me to appreciate and value what I have instead of what I haven't. Today is what you have. In terms of health and living each day, when you see people your age dying, I think how lucky I am. I can walk out of here and enjoy the sunshine.'


Eight weeks after Tony Dimattina's death I am sitting in the lounge at McCulloch House when Angelina and Rosina arrive. A 'broken heart' seems a trite description, but if you have known someone with a broken heart, or had one yourself, you know the words are a perfect fit. So it is with Angelina and Rosina. Their manner is dignified but their hearts are broken. They are at McCulloch House because the care given to families of the deceased doesn't end with the patient's death.

I have seen pictures of Tony. He was handsome. A genial man with a strong body and a face of kindness and integrity, he's the sort of man about whom women complain there aren't enough made to go around. For Angelina, his death is like dying herself. In fact, since his death, her health has deteriorated. She suffers lower-body pain just as Tony himself had.

Today she has been at Monash Medical Centre for tests before coming to McCulloch House to see Dr Peter Martin. In addition to her physical pain she is afflicted with scruples and doubts. Could she have done things differently? Could she have done more?

Peter Martin is in his early thirties. At first palliative care seems an unusual professional choice for this black-haired Irish Protestant who came to Australia from Belfast in 1993. He is a lover of life, a gourmet cook and a connoisseur of fine wines and single-malt whiskies. Yet he seems to easily cope with the difficult aspects of dying, buoyed by the challenge and his respect for the uniqueness of people. Right now he is listening thoughtfully as Angelina pours out her heart. He sits next to her on the small couch, his body turned directly to her, his eyes on her tear-splashed face.

Sometimes the bereaved partner in a long-term marriage suffers a sort of symbolic dying, a process of actual physical pain akin to that suffered by the deceased. The pain is real. It expresses the dying of the relationship and the changes that are occurring. At the moment Peter is concerned only with the psychological pain that Angelina is expressing. Any other consideration is up to the doctor who has just done the medical tests at Monash Medical Centre. Sitting by her on the couch, his body turned towards her and his eyes looking into hers he says simply, 'It's normal to have these thoughts and feelings. It's normal to ask questions.'

Angelina shakes her head. 'I can't sleep. I feel such pain.'

'That, too, is normal,' he reassures her. 'Some people feel they are going mad. You looked after Tony all your life.'

His recognition and validation of their loving relationship comforts Angelina a little. 'Yes, always he want me to wash him, always his wife. But, Doctor…' There is a long pause. Peter waits with no air of waiting. 'Doctor, if you did not put that tube in, maybe, would he…?'

'I'm glad you asked that question,' Peter responds. This doesn't arise from tact or manipulation, but from a genuine interest in learning the specific cause of Angelina's additional pain. 'We discussed it with you and Tony—to put it down the gullet or into his side directly into the stomach. He didn't want it in his stomach.'

'Michael, Dr Ashby, he no want to do it. Tony want it, but not in his stomach.'

'Tony wanted a feeding tube,' Peter agrees. He doesn't say how despairing he and Michael had felt about it, how they had to consciously respect Tony's right, no matter how futile, to have the treatment he wanted. 'We decided on the stomach. The reason they phoned you to come over that night, Angelina, was to make sure Tony was in agreement to have it in his stomach. We took a risk. We knew he wanted it down his gullet, but if we had put it there and it hadn't worked, we wouldn't have been able to put one into his stomach.'

'He never say, "I want to die."' Angelina murmurs. It is impossible to say whether her remark is a general observation or whether it relates to the feeding tube.

'The cancer had spread everywhere, Angelina,' Peter says. 'It was all around his bottom and stomach. His lungs were filled with spots the size of plums.'

'Seven years my husband sick,' Angelina says.

Funny, I think, how we describe cancer in fruit and vegetable sizes: cancer the size of plums, a tumour like a small orange or a big grapefruit, a node like a lemon, a growth like a pea.

'He had colorectal cancer, cancer in the large bowel,' Peter tells Angelina, his voice warm but firm. 'For most of these cancers, people don't know they have them. Tony probably had it in his early forties. He probably had it for ten or fifteen years. We did our best. You will always miss Tony.'

When I consider the state of Antonio Dimattina's body when he died, it is no wonder that society keeps death and dying under wraps. Dying is not an easy process for many people, and for a few it is terrible. That is the reality. We have been so softened by the comforts of technology and protected from nature's potential savagery that our view of life allows no place for suffering. But that isn't the only reason the demand for euthanasia is so widespread. It is widespread because the agony and mess of some 'natural' deaths fly in the face of all we have previously known or experienced about life. They are shocking. They are beyond our ability to deal with. To take our own life or that of a loved one in these extreme circumstances seems a reasonable and rational act.

For rationalists, Antonio Dimattina would be the perfect candidate for euthanasia. However, he was born a Catholic and stayed one. He believed his life was a gift from God, something to be looked after until it was taken from him. His belief probably ran along old-fashioned lines—a spatial God up in the heavens or somewhere 'out there'. When his daughter became blind, and when he became ill, Tony continued to trust in God. He didn't endure what he did to throw his faith away in preference for a 'rational' act.

Is there any way in which it would have been better if Tony had embraced the means of ending it all himself? Is there value in relying on a mystery to give one strength? Is life pointless without mystery? Or is life merely a matter of being born, loving, hating, suffering, rejoicing, and then sliding off the planet into nothingness? Is there a value in belief, a rationality in belief, a finessing of thought that heightens our sensitivity to things worthy of honouring and helps us separate them from those worthy of contempt? Is it worthwhile opting to believe that at death we don't fall off into nothingness, and that we can't choose our own time for going?

Somewhere in the course of his own personal journey Tony decided to find his strength in mystery. He chose, at whatever subconscious level, a seemingly irrational stance in preference to a wholly rational view of life. Maybe he stuck to his faith because he hadn't found modern life all that rational anyway. In taking this stance he gave full play to a different form of rationality in his life—a strong faith in a creator. Had he acted 'reasonably and rationally' by everyday standards, he would have had to kill himself before his suffering became extreme because, having reached that point, reason and rationality had nothing to offer. Tony's religious faith provided a framework of order, form and meaning.

Where do I stand? My time at McCulloch House is running out and I am beginning to feel like a coward, a white-knuckled wimp whose only decision is not to make one. The inadequacy of my initial question—*Is euthanasia necessary or could accessible palliative care supplant the need for it?*—is disconcertingly obvious. I had blissfully believed it struck at the heart of the problem. Now it seems limited, skewed, even naive. If Tony Dimattina had requested euthanasia, who on God's earth would have the legal or moral right to deny it to him?

It is clear now that I am not dealing exclusively with palliative care or euthanasia, or with the problem of suffering, of belief, or of that old chestnut—the meaning of life. I am dealing with choice.

Tony Dimattina could have found some means of committing suicide had he wished. He chose to endure. But his endurance was possible only because his pain was sufficiently controlled by palliative care. If a person has faith—not a faith of simplistic rules but an authentic relationship between themselves and God—couldn't submitting to seven years of progressive painful deterioration alter one's perception of what that faith is or what it requires? If Tony hadn't had palliative care, would he have chosen to endure? Palliative care gave him a choice, enabling him to choose what, without palliative care, would have been unendurable.

What of the person who has no faith, or whose faith is such that euthanasia is acceptable? I remember Harry Symonds's simple trust in 'the fella upstairs' juxtaposed with his strong belief in euthanasia, and Yvonne Linden's belief in euthanasia and an afterlife. What if someone wants out of their suffering and another person is in a position to help him or her? (I am talking here about the terminally ill and those in *profound* pain.) You can't feel in your own mind or body how much the terminally ill person is suffering. You can only believe they are suffering in a way you would find very difficult yourself. If a patient clearly chooses to be put out of their agony and a doctor believes it is morally acceptable to do so, from where does an *observer* draw his or her right to intrude? From semi-academic religious books? How much easier to have a second-hand attitude than trying to determine oneself what is right!

When I consider Tony's choice, I am reminded of Joseph Campbell's Hero's Journey. Now, whenever I hear the expression 'death with dignity', Antonio Dimattina is the first person who comes to mind.

# Last Rites

*Since ev'ry man who lives is born to die,*
*And no one can boast sincere felicity,*
*With equal mind, what happens, let us bear,*
*Nor joy nor grieve too much for things beyond our care.*
*Like pilgrims to th' appointed place we tend;*
*The world's an inn, and death the journey's end.*
  —John Dryden, 'Palamon and Arcite'

'Would you like to wash your mother's body?' a nurse might one day ask our middle-aged children while we lie there, newly dead and free from any concern about who does what to whom. We might even become the object of a final sibling row when the nurse asks, 'What clothes would you like me to dress your partner/husband/father in?'

Such are the thoughts that go through my mind one day when I see a man and two women carry several freshly dry-cleaned suits into a room where the patient, a Greek gentleman, is close to death. Later I learn that the patient carefully chose his own 'laying out' outfit, including tie and socks. This knowledge makes me realise how little I know about what actually happens in the moments following death, which palliative caregivers consider a highly sensitive and critical time for the bereaved.

McCulloch House has no refrigeration room, so bodies are removed by ambulance to a funeral home within a few hours of death. The changes after death are very individual. Some people look normal; others quickly turn grey or black. Some bodies stay fresh for a few hours; others have an odour even before death that becomes stronger immediately after. These are part of the end-of-life realities from which we have become, quite happily, separated, although not without some cost. Such realities, when totally unexpected, compound the trauma of loss.

For the family there is a small 'quiet room', a centre with a few chairs where one can sit in undisturbed silence and think, meditate, or pray in peace. On a few occasions families have requested use of this room for a brief 'laying out' and 'visiting'. So it was with the Greek gentleman. Dressed in the black suit he had chosen, he lay for an hour in the meditation room, looking sartorially splendid—as he knew he would—and surrounded by dozens of animated friends and admirers. So ebullient was the mourning crowd that I was reminded of my mother's elderly, confused friend who, on leaving my mother's funeral, described it as the loveliest wedding she had ever been to.

Before the body is removed there are tasks to be done. Despite Hollywood, most of us die with our eyes open. So the first thing is to close the eyes. If there is a drip, or a catheter, the needle or tube must be removed. After this the bedclothes might have to be changed or rearranged, towels and medications removed. Does the family want to stay while this is happening? Do they want to watch, go and look out the window, help do it themselves, or disappear to play golf? What role they play, if any, will be up to them.

At McCulloch House there is ample space for the bereaved

to remain in the room and assist in small ways. Here again the situation differs from most deaths in an acute-care hospital. Saying goodbye properly to the deceased, of which laying out is a part, can help a bereaved person accept the reality of death. Laying out and washing is an intimate act. Some patients make a specific request that it be done by a certain nurse or family member. They have felt loved in life by that person and want more of that love even after death.

Apart from the bodies being washed, the hair will be combed and tidied, false teeth put in, glasses put on or removed, hands folded in rest and bedclothes straightened. Many people still feel connected to the body and see these moments as a last chance to do something for it. This caring ritual slows down the final goodbye. It is a chance, too, for family to become aware of their real feelings—anger perhaps at the memory of the long weeks of illness, the physically exhausting weeks of care and the demands made on everyone.

Some people will be too repulsed or frightened to touch the cooling body. They would like to help, but can't, so will let the nurse take care of everything. Just choosing the fresh nightgown or pyjamas—even doing nothing and watching the ritual—can help mitigate the finality of death. Some people want nothing to do with any of it and are out the door in a shot once death has occurred.

These rites are a fond ceremony of farewell for those who remain rather than those who have gone. Hence this old ritual is still practised today as a source of comfort for the bereaved.

After the body is cleaned one last time, making it as fresh and attractive as possible, the nurse or family dresses it. Some will have chosen what they wish to wear. Most will leave it up to the family. Considering what happens in the crematorium or graveyard, the way one is outfitted seems irrelevant. However, for some bereaved the clothes chosen for burial signify their perception of who and what we were in life. Emotions can be so raw at this stage that even this choice can trigger conflict. A woman might have chosen her favourite slacks but her partner loves a certain cocktail dress and her daughter holds out for the lounge robe she sewed. A man might request a tracksuit, but his wife thinks a business suit better, and his sons can't see what is wrong with pyjamas. If there is to be a funeral—and not immediate cremation with a memorial service held at a later date—the final choice is usually not made until the corpse is at the mortuary.

When Joan's mother, Linda Evans, died at McCulloch House, Joan left immediately. She had reached the front door when something made her stop and return. This short story is about sisters and saying a proper goodbye.

'Mum was married at seventeen and had the first of three babies at eighteen,' says Joan, a striking woman with sporty clothes and thirteen rings on her fingers. We are sitting in my favourite spot, the settee in the McCulloch House lounge that backs onto the glass of a floor-to-ceiling window and affords an overview of what is going on.

'My older sister, Becky, and I never had any real friendship. Dad was very interested in sports, and so was Becky. I wasn't. They had that in common. I was very aware of that as a child, this happy link between my sister and my dad, which I didn't have. When Becky grew up and married she went to live in Queensland. In time she had six children.

'There's been a fair bit of cancer in my family. My dad died at fifty-six with lung cancer and my brother died at thirty-one with a lymphoma. My aunt Shirley died at sixty-eight of a cancer-related operation. She had a tortured, tormented death, absolutely horrible, and all they wanted to give her was Panadol!' Pausing for a moment, Joan points to some rings on her fingers. 'That's my brother's wedding ring, that's my mother's, that's my own.

'When Dad died, I was there for Mum. Becky wasn't. Becky was off in Queensland. Mum was my best friend, but it was me who had the responsibility. I taught Mum ceramics and cross-words, and how to occupy her spare time so she wouldn't be lonely. When I had my last child, Brad, who's nine now, I was very ill and Mum had sole responsibility for him for his first three months. We were very close.

'Mum kept having this throat problem. She lived in Bendigo, and the doctor told her she had a virus and should take some Panadol. It didn't get any better and she saw a specialist. He told her she had cancer in her upper chest and it was closing over her throat. He gave her eight weeks to live, but she lived for eighteen months. She had radiotherapy right away, and it was fabulously successful. Well, at least her voice got back to normal and she felt fine.

'I arranged for someone in Bendigo to call her every morning between seven and seven-thirty to make sure she was all right, and gave three people keys to her door. The doctor was visiting her one day and found her collapsed. She had an alternative—to go as a private patient and get a biopsy in two days, or go as an outpatient and wait two weeks. She took the two-weeks option. When I phoned Becky, she said, "Mum knows. She's just putting off getting the final result."

'When Mum got the final results, she didn't return immediately to Bendigo but spent the time comforting me. The only thing she said was, "I wanted to be around when Brad grew up." Other than that, she didn't question it, didn't blame anyone. She went home to Bendigo and had palliative care there, as my dad had. She was still driving but felt very tired. Finally she closed the house.

'McCulloch House had been only open a week when she first came in. She had a total fear of hospitals and was petrified of being put into Dandenong Hospital. But when she went through the doors of McCulloch House, she said the place was so peaceful that she could die happily there.'

When Becky arrived from Queensland to help, the detritus of the past floated to the surface. 'Mum was so thrilled to have Becky here, so terribly happy. Having Becky meant everything to her. I felt pushed to the side. I'd done a lot, I'd always been there for Mum, and it seemed I didn't count like Becky counted. I felt really put out. It was very hurtful. But a wonderful thing has come out of Mum's death. My sister and I now have an unbelievably beautiful relationship.'

'How did that happen?' I ask.

'During Mum's last illness, Becky went back and forth to Queensland. And I finally realised how hard it was for her to leave her husband and six children. I'd been so caught up in our childhood relationship I hadn't realised how much time had gone by, how things had changed. So I made a point when Mum wanted something done of letting Becky do it. Just out of that simple thing, it all came right.

'The atmosphere of this place helped. It's so, well, reconciling. Like when Mum got near the end, we were sleeping here and having meals. I mean, it was wonderful. But at one stage Becky, who is volatile, was rude and threatening to the staff. The next day nothing was said. Not a word. It was as though nothing had happened. That struck both of us, the amazing way, the really loving way, the staff handled it.

'When Mum was here, we asked the nurses, "Why can't you

put her out of her misery?" But really, she wasn't in misery. We were. It was us who wanted her given a shot. I believe very strongly in euthanasia. Mum came home for her twenty-fifth wedding anniversary. She asked me to kill her. She didn't have money, only a rental house. Pride was the only thing she had and she was losing it. She was constipated and I had to put in suppositories. She kept saying, "Oh, you shouldn't have to be doing that." She wanted to end her life so she wouldn't be a drag on the family. She couldn't cope with my emptying the commode. I wouldn't kill my mother. I couldn't. But I could kill someone else's mother. I think those politicians who've stopped it [euthanasia] in the Northern Territory are awful. But when I saw how Mum died here, there wasn't any need of it.'

On the night Linda died a nurse told the sisters that it might be best not to touch their mother when they went in.

'This made me very angry, but later Irene [a nurse] said Mum was deep down into dying, her breathing stopping and starting, and had we hugged her she might have struggled against it and tried to come on up. I wasn't frightened of death, but I was frightened of life without my mother. Irene was unbelievable. She talked to Mum throughout her dying with so much compassion. As soon as Mum died, I left the room to go home. I wanted to escape, to be out of there. But Irene caught up with me by the front door. She simply said, "I want you to say goodbye to your mother properly."

'I went back into the room and took Mum's hand. When I laid my head on Mum's chest, she exhaled. Irene put her arm around me and reassured me so I wouldn't be frightened. Irene then asked what were Mum's favourite pyjamas. I took my time and said a proper goodbye. Afterwards this meant a lot to me. I was pleased I'd gone back, pleased I'd picked out the pyjamas for her.'

After a moment, Joan asks, 'Are you going to write about Mum? If you do, I'd like you to say what a wonderful cook she was. She always cooked with a wood stove and everything tasted beautiful. My daughter wanted me to make the same rock-cake Mum made, but when I looked for Mum's recipe book, I couldn't find it. Finally it turned up. And all the recipes said "a pinch of this" or "a few of that" or "a small handful" of whatever. There wasn't a recipe in it I could follow. Becky and I really laughed about that. Knowing Mum died surrounded by so much love and compassion has sort of freed our good memories and allowed us to let go of the bad. If she'd died the way my aunt did, I'd never have recovered.'

I am sitting at the big polished table in the lounge where Irene has been going through a patient's record with a third-year student nurse, who is on a two-week rotation in palliative care. Irene is the only trained enrolled nurse on staff. An enrolled nurse has completed all basic nursing care but has less academic training. Born in Colac in the western district of Victoria fifty-seven years ago, Irene and her policeman husband have always been heavily involved in their community, particularly in the Meals on Wheels program.

'I've been a nurse for twenty-five years and in palliative care for ten, nine of them at Bethlehem Hospital,' she says. 'They do their best at Bethlehem, but when I came here I saw it wasn't only a door opening for me, but a door opening for all of Victoria. In some nursing homes old people die in rows of sixteen. Care of the dying aged is changing because palliative care has shown us what can be done. But there's just not enough of anything in some of those older nursing homes to help people have good deaths.

'We bring in patients and relatives to assess McCulloch House before they're placed here. Some patients arrive very fearful, wondering if they'll be given something to make them die. At Monash they have been told, "There's nothing more we can do for you." They're given a tour of this place, and after it they seem to melt into the facility.

'This is where I see the hostess in me coming out,' Irene remarks. 'I say to them, "You're here for the right reasons." And they might respond with something like, "Well, Dad was driving the car three days ago." So I get the message, which is, "Please keep him going." But there's a point where you have to make them aware of what will happen soon. When the patient's condition changes we might say, "We have a pastoral-care worker, or a social worker, is there anything you'd like to tap into?" That gives everyone a chance to air their concerns.

'I believe it's good for the family to have small tasks to do. For instance, I make sure they know how to keep the patient's mouth moist. I'll put some music in the background and get the family to do some gentle massage. I'll bring in aromatherapy. We have an electric burner and choose lavender as a relaxant, and bergamot. It isn't all gloom by a long shot. One night, for example, a wife and daughter stayed overnight, so I went and tucked them both in, saying, "I've tucked Dad in, so I might as well tuck you in too." When the man died, I said that he should go out in state. He'd played for the Melbourne Football Club. I put the football scarf around his neck and a little fighting gorilla with boxing gloves on his chest. There was laughter in the room. I told the family to keep talking, that their dad could hear. It was an opportunity for them all to say goodbye. It was a good death.

'Both my mum and dad were from pioneer stock. They had to do without a lot of things they couldn't afford and became very strong. I've got that strength and their strong sense of hospitality. I'm "old Victoria". I like to make people feel warm, welcome, and at home. I ask the patient what he or she would like to be called, and 99 per cent of the time they say their first name. I like to take formality out of what goes on around here.

'I have deep spiritual beliefs. Euthanasia is thrown at me a lot by relatives. I simply say, "I understand how hard it is for you to be witnessing this." Sometimes the patient says, "I hate it. I don't want to be here." They are extremely angry, angry at God, angry at everyone. I try to get them to redirect their anger at cancer, not the people surrounding it. Mostly I tell the family to touch their mum or dad and say how much they loved them, and what they loved about the things they did for them. Touch is so very important, but some people find it hard to do.'


Because palliative care has a pronounced spiritual component, does it attract health professionals whose own spiritual or religious values involuntarily spill over into the care of the patient? In their desire to comfort the patient, do some caregivers find the need to proselytise irresistible? I haven't seen any evidence of this, but then how would I know? My time at McCulloch House is limited, and generally confined to daylight hours. This question of whether subtle proselytising occurs is critically important to me. I can't imagine a worse fate than to be weak and subject to the type of psychological religious pressure I endured as a child. It seems to me that many people might share my fear. I recall the defensive initial reaction of the Dilorenzo family when a priest arrived, ostensibly without a specific invitation, at Eva Dilorenzo's bedside.

I seek out the head honcho in these parts, Jill, the unit-nurse manager. Jill is the type of human being whose very person sums up what an organisation is all about. Wise, affable, under-standing, and deceptively low-keyed in voice and movement, Jill is the linchpin that holds together the daily running of the centre. She has Australia-wide experience in palliative care, staff management and hospital administration. As part of the original team she was responsible for most of the hiring at McCulloch House.

'What we've tried to establish here,' Jill says, 'and I think we've succeeded, is, in Michael's [Ashby] words, "a respectful democracy". We let people be who they are and it works. If a nurse feels relaxed, the patients feel that, too. No one around here discusses their own religious views, I'm pretty sure of that. If the patient wants to know what they are, the nurse would probably say so. It's not really an issue. If a staff member was going around pushing their own religious beliefs onto patients I'd ask them to stop. If they kept on, they'd have to leave.

'What we have is a group of people with quite different ideas about certain bioethical problems. Some feel euthanasia's a good thing, others are strongly opposed, and still others aren't sure how they feel. Some believe in God, some are agnostic, and I suppose there are a few atheists. They were hired because they're very good at what they do and can work as a member of a team. They weren't vetted for their religious beliefs. So if there's a team looking after a patient, you'd find a variety of views, a check-and-balance system, although it wasn't set up that way. This helps ensure that no one's going to dun some poor patient with their own religious beliefs.'

Suddenly Jill chuckles. It is a nice, low yuk-yuk. 'Actually, I remember we did have an incident along those lines. One of the staff whose job is to lend a hand around the place was visit-ing a patient and holding forth at length about death, sin and resurrection. In general he was preaching the Bible. As soon as

I heard that, I went looking for him. In the meantime the patient had died. While looking, I ran into the patient's family.

'They showed me a small gift and a beautiful card they had bought for this staff member. They raved about how wonderful he was, what a consolation, what a support! Said they couldn't have managed without him. And here I was on my way to tell him to knock it off!'

Behind her glasses Jill's eyes glitter with mirth. 'It was a timely reminder that it takes all sorts. In a place like this where there's always an undercurrent of emotion, needs, like water, seem to flow to their own level.'

# Grief and Love

*Grief is itself a medicine.*
— William Cowper, 'Charity'

At eighty-three William 'Bill' Jackson is still a handsome man: straight-backed, silver-haired, conservatively dressed in a navy blazer, grey slacks and silk tie. Looking at him as he amiably chats with the people around him, you would never guess at the effort he is making to cover the way he is hurting. That is probably true for most of the crowd now seated in semicircular rows in the McCulloch House lounge. Although it is night and midweek, the room is packed. It has been important for everyone to dress with care to honour this occasion, to mark this milestone in the journey through loss. In a few minutes Sandra, the pastoral-care worker, will start a memorial service of remembrance and thanksgiving for all who have died at McCulloch House within the past six months.

The atmosphere, although edgy, is bright, expectant, with occasional laughter cutting through the buzz of voices. People meet, shake hands, hug, and children run freely. Pots of fat white and yellow chrysanthemums clutter the mantel and shelves. Thirty-five names are listed in the program handed out by volunteers, and among the names I see that of Bill's wife, Janet. I had met Bill at his home a week or so earlier. 'I cry every day,' he had told me with a simplicity that carried the awful weight of losing your mate when you are old. Almost out of time yourself, recovery time is virtually nonexistent.

The service starts, simple, non-denominational, non-sentimental.

> Spirit of God,
> brooding over the waters
> of our chaos,
> inspire us to generous living.
>
> Wind of God,
> dancing over the desert
> of our reluctance,
> lead us to the oasis of celebration.
>
> Breath of God,
> inspiring communication
> among strangers,
> make us channels
> of your peace.

Then Barbara reads from Ecclesiastes.

> There is a time for everything,
> And a season for every activity under heaven:
> A time to be born and a time to die,

A time to plant and a time to uproot,
A time to kill and a time to heal…

This is followed by a couple of poems, a psalm, a Judaic prayer, a passage by Henry Scott-Holland, and a translation of the Lord's Prayer from Syriac–Aramaic that are read by staff members.

As Sandra reads each deceased's name, a family member or friend walks to the front, lights a candle and places it upright in a deep tray of sand. Although tears flow, everyone gives themselves completely to the last prayers and final song. A quality, like a mirage of light-heartedness, short-lived but invigorating, fills the silence at the end.

The entire service takes forty-five minutes. Coffee and tea are served and, although tissues are passed around and noses are loudly blown, there is animated talk and a sense of relief and restoration. The bereaved aren't only remembering their dead— they're also struggling to restore themselves to life. They know the respect that people's feelings are accorded within palliative care. Feelings aren't considered to exist on a lower plane than reason. You are 'allowed' to feel whatever it is you feel—rage against the cancer, anger at the beloved for deserting you, relief they have finally died, grief that breaks the heart—and it is thought healthy to acknowledge that feeling, even if only to oneself.

Because palliative care doesn't seek to cure the patient but addresses the range of problems that a terminally ill person and their loved ones can suffer, the social and psychological support it offers continues for a while after death—in the case of McCulloch House for a year after the patient's death.

The day after the memorial service I speak to Wendy. In pre-politically correct days Wendy, who assists with the bereavement program, would have been described as a willowy blue-eyed blonde with a million-dollar smile. She has packed a lot into her life so far—a bachelor of science degree, studies in ethics and theology, marriage, motherhood and a variety of work experience. Prior to joining McCulloch House, Wendy was a funeral director, an experience she describes as 'stressful' but one that took her into every level of the local community 'from dumpy rooms in Collingwood to mansions in Toorak'.

Wendy tells me the bereavement program starts with a file card for each patient with address of next-of-kin, and the soliciting of a volunteer staff member to follow that particular family.

'When a patient dies we notify all agencies who have had contact with them or their family. During the first week, we send a card to the next-of-kin, saying, "The staff at McCulloch House is thinking of you and we'd love to hear from you if we can help in any way." After three months I pull the card and ask the staff member to please give the family a ring or to write. If it's a family having particular difficulties, then Barbara calls. A note is then made on the card as to status. At six months the family is invited to attend a memorial service. As the first anniversary approaches, we send a note saying something like, "Thinking of you on so-and-so's anniversary." Then, after the first year, we write a handwritten letter to say that if the family ever wishes to drop by, they'd be welcome.'

I remark that I often observe her at the front door greeting new patients, and that several patients have mentioned that her bubbly welcome helped with the desolation they felt on arrival. 'I want patients and their families to feel welcome and at home,' she says. 'They're so brave.' The last two words are emphasised. 'When I took this job, I decided to stamp it with my own character. I created my job myself. You can do that here. You're not expected to be anyone but yourself. There's space here to be young. Some people think this is an old-age home. They can't get the idea that young people die too.'

I wonder what difference the bereavement program has made. I think of Bill Jackson. He comes to mind because Barbara mentioned how one loss brings up another. And Phillip the nurse had said something similar: 'What's in the past really isn't in the past. It's real today.' Bill's losses weren't extraordinary—in fact they were almost typical for his generation—but what his life demonstrates is the large role loss plays in even the most ordinary life.

'I was born in England,' Bill says at the small kitchen table nestled against the back wall of his Dandenong home. From the large window at my side there is a long-range view of rolling hills, red roofs and gum trees. The house is warm. The rain has stopped. Everything glistens. I help myself to another slice of cake while Bill makes a pot of tea.

'My dad went to war when I was about two years old,' Bill tells me. 'He was gassed on the Somme, and when he was thirty-five he died because of the damage to his lungs. Eventually my mother met someone, but he was a Roman Catholic and his wife wouldn't give him a divorce.' Bill puts the teapot on the table and says with proud emphasis, 'As soon as his wife died, though, he married my mother.'

Obviously Bill still takes pride in the fidelity of his long-dead stepfather and the dignity of his long-dead mother. Again I am struck, chastened, by the way in which our behaviour towards one another endures; as if our actions, long forgotten by us, create images that fly out and impale themselves in the minds of others. Mentally I note Shakespeare's oft-quoted lines that the evil men do lives after them while 'the good is oft interred with their bones', and think he must have been having a bad day.

'I got married at twenty-one,' Bill continues. 'My wife was eighteen. I joined the army and went off to India, to Ranchi.

My wife showed a great indifference to me. I'd wait a month for a letter overseas. We moved to Australia in 1951 and divorced eighteen years later. We had five sons, but she didn't give me a happy life. I worked as a bricklayer, did well, and retired quite early.

'In September 1969 I went back to England to visit my sister on the old P&O liner *Canberra*. Janet, who was to become my wife, boarded the ship in Los Angeles. I was fifty-six. She was fifty-six too, and had been a war widow for twenty-eight years. Her two sons had told her when she got on the ship, "Do what you like, but don't come back with some old Pom."' At this point Bill chuckles. 'That's exactly what she did do. In six months we were married and she came to live in Melbourne.

'We had a wonderful life together, always in agreement, and we couldn't do enough for each other. She had been alone a long time, and I had been so unhappy in my first marriage. Being together was just wonderful. I told her right at the beginning, "I will never do anything to cause you unhappiness or grief." Bill's voice is slightly tremulous as he stands staring out the kitchen window. Then he says briskly, 'She was a very well-organised, always pleasant woman. She worked at McEwans in dinner services, liked nice things, and kept the house beautiful.

'Sometimes I'd say to her after she got sick, "Don't worry. I'll go before you." But she died of ovarian cancer. It came on without warning. She went down so thin. It was terrible to watch her. The specialist told her, "I can't cure you, but I can arrest it." Janet was a realistic woman though. She marked all her bits and pieces and got ready a long while before she died. Her boys have all her crystal and the tall Mary McGregor pink Venetian glass. She always said she had no pain. She wasn't on drugs until the last few days, then they gave her morphine.

'I think euthanasia is good, but I didn't discuss it with her.

On the last day Robert, the nurse, said, "You know what is happening, Janet?" She said she did. She then said what hymns she wanted and what church, and asked to be cremated. I slept at McCulloch House for five days, had all my meals there. Her two sons and their wives were there. Watching her go, I held her hand and didn't cry at all. She never complained, you see, not one bit, so I couldn't sit there and cry. She praised all the girls here, Eileen and Phyllis and the rest. Right at the end she said, "I love you." It was 1 a.m. We left right away. I was all right until the day of the funeral. I stood there greeting every-one, thanking them for coming. I was all right until I got into the church and saw the coffin.

'I cry every day. I used to say to Janet that we'll see each other again. That's our belief if we're Christians, isn't it? It helps a little, but not really. People don't think about these things until they experience it themselves. I didn't even know what palliative care was. They treat you so nice at McCulloch House. It's the greeting you get at the door. They see you coming up the path and are waiting when you arrive. The quality of care was a big surprise. Nothing was too much trouble for them. They never got fed up. It still goes on, the caring. A nurse has popped by four times since Janet left. The first time she brought me a yard of chocolate, then an Easter egg and then a bottle of beer her son had brewed. Then the two nurses, John and Phillip, used to come around.

'I wear Janet's wedding ring on a chain around my neck. I keep the house as nice as I can. It's fair to say that I'm lonely. That's to be expected, isn't it? It's been good having people from McCulloch House pop around or phone me. Being thoughtful like that helps you keep going, helps you to keep in touch with normal life. '

The Centre for Grief Education is located on the second floor of the old McCulloch House building. It is financed by a government grant, and although it is entirely independent from the palliative-care centre, the course offered in counselling the bereaved—four hours a week for thirty weeks—supports the palliative-care belief that caring for a patient's family doesn't stop the moment death occurs. Some bereaved need more support than is offered by follow-up letters and phone calls.

The video I am watching in the featureless seminar room is *Hard Medicine,* a skilful documentary on loss and grief. When Linda, the centre's education co-ordinator arrives, she tells me that many people need to tell their own story but often find they can't. Watching this video, which articulates the confusion of other bereaved people who have suffered loss and who feel thrown into chaos or simply mad, makes it easier for others to express their own feelings.

'For a while after a death there's a convergence of people helping out, washing the car, walking the dog, bringing casseroles,' says Linda, a bright-eyed young woman whose ample figure lends her a touch of substance and grandeur. 'But after some weeks the support drops off,' she continues. 'Casseroles don't come any more, the flowers are all dead, the phone rarely rings, and the bereaved is left alone. And then they think they are going crazy.

'Husbands contact us and say, "It's been three months, six months, since our daughter died, and my wife isn't getting any better, in fact, she's getting worse." Or a woman might say, "My sister has changed. It's been eighteen months since her baby died. She used to be the life of the party, but she won't come to family functions. When is she going to get back to normal?" In both those cases you've got double grief—the husband for his wife and child, the sister for her sister and her deceased infant niece or nephew.'

Grieving is something that all of us do sooner or later in life, yet the behaviour and states of mind that it induces only recently have been studied as a subject.

'Grief challenges and frightens us,' Linda says. 'It's chaotic, and we like control and predictability. A lot of our avoidance in facing grief is our inability to watch someone else in pain and endure the discomfort. We say to ourselves, "What can I say? What can I do?" We feel helpless and hopeless...But we have to simply *be*, allow ourselves to be touched by it. To come through it you must go through it. But the messages around us don't permit it.

'We've developed this special language. People are shushed from crying. "There, there, it's OK," we say. We pass a tissue and tell people to dry their eyes. After a while our attitude to those grieving is "Buck up and get on with it." There's a general feeling that getting upset is bad for you. We suggest they don't "dwell" on that. We speak of passing on or crossing over and avoid factual words like 'died'.

'Time can heighten the sense of missing,' Linda points out. 'You can miss more, but miss differently. The deceased isn't here physically, but the relationship hasn't died. A lot of people, about 20 per cent, are at risk of complicated grief, grief that they can't move away from or integrate. They feel cut off from themselves. They can't function properly at home or work and they avoid their friends. They need help to move on and relocate their beloved in a new, more comfortable place in their new world without them.

'One thing we are specifically doing is trying to educate doctors and nurses to facilitate the grieving process by encouraging patients to express their doubts and fears. An enormous number of people are drugged, tranquillised, at their beloved's funeral. We do what we can to dodge pain, but it's a false hope. Pain has to be dealt with, and that's what this centre is all about.'

Brendan is in charge of McCulloch House's volunteer-training program. An ebullient, ponytailed thirty-seven he has done graduate work in counselling psychology, is a jazz buff and a book addict and is involved in 'playback theatre', where real-life audience stories are acted out.

After weeks of trying to set up a meeting with Brendan, I run into him in the Monash Medical Centre library. We decide the meeting is fortuitous and go to the staff cafeteria for a brief interview. The volunteer program is important in the McCulloch House way of doing things, and I am curious about what a volunteer can contribute to a dying person or their relatives, and who would volunteer for such work.

When I say this, Brendan laughs. 'Young people find death both fascinating and scary. And they're interested in what scares them. When I advertised for volunteers, I specified that they all be undergraduate health students, and most of them are, although we have a couple of super older people. I thought maybe I'd get two or three replies, but I got twenty-five. What do I look for? I expect people to have good, selfish reasons for coming here. Psychology training in Australia gives very little hands-on placement experience. This isn't only a good learning experience but looks good on your CV. When someone comes here and says, "I want to help other people," that's when I get suspicious.

'As far as the program goes, I'm inventing it as we go along. The first thing we do is get to know each other. We play a few games and get the volunteers used to accepting applause and some praise. Most people are very used to seeing where we strike out, but we're very poor in naming what we do well and we're absolutely no good at all in accepting praise.

'Being able to accept praise is very important. No matter how successful we are, we then dismiss it as ordinary. "Nothing at all," we say dismissively after we've done something well for a patient. Or if a patient pays a compliment, we might refute what they've said in an attempt to be modest and say, "I don't think so." This makes patients feel cut out, as if their opinions and views aren't important and they aren't involved in what's going on. So one of the things volunteers are taught is how to respond to a patient's thankfulness by saying something like, "I'm glad I helped you." It's very simple stuff, but this is a very sensitive and critical time in people's lives.'

Volunteers meet once a month, and after every shift write what they have done and how they felt about it. They also note any challenges or problems they have had and whether there were ways to handle things differently.

Brendan laughs. 'As to what we actually do, we do anything that's needed. Maybe wheel a patient over to the main building for a church service, or sit and read to them, make phone calls or write a letter they dictate, give a manicure or a pedicure, or comfort the relatives after a death. Massage is a very important part of our caring—just simple hand or foot massage. The patients love it.'

Brendan pauses, then sighs. 'A couple of older women actually have cried. They've never had that sort of loving, personal attention. Once one of our young volunteers was massaging an old woman's feet when the patient started crying. The volunteer asked if she were sad, and the woman replied, "It's the first time in my life anyone has ever touched me without wanting sex." It hit me where I live when I heard that, made me realise the impact simple things have when the caring's straight from the heart and there's some laughter waiting in the wings.'

# Freedom from Pain

*When vain desire at last and vain regret*
*Go hand in hand to death, and all is vain,*
*What shall assuage the unforgotten pain*
*And teach the unforgetful to forget?*
—Dante Gabriel Rossetti, 'The One Hope'

It is 9 a.m. and we are at rounds. Fourteen of us seated at the grand oak table in the McCulloch House conference room waiting for everyone to arrive. This is where staff members review the patient caseload, exchange information and make decisions. Rounds are invaluable to me as an opportunity to view how the staff thinks and works. I cherish the insights that flesh out the facts and love the flashes of wit and compassion that erupt from time to time. They reveal a commonalty of goal—to relieve the pain of others—and as I haven't been part of a professional group before that is willing to put ego, power plays, and grandstanding aside, I find the experience energising.

Nurse Sharon enters with her sharpei puppy, Devo—McCulloch House's new mascot. Devo trots briskly around the room as if checking on attendance before settling down under the table as the rest of the group arrives.

Dr Stuart Moir presents the cases. Stuart, a youthful-looking twenty-six, is doing a three-month rotation in palliative care as part of his residency for physician training. He chooses from a pile of folders in front of him and plunges into an updated summary of the patients' medical condition. As he goes through the list, my gut tightens on hearing the full extent of cancer's malignant ability to find a home within the hidden nooks and crannies of the human body. Behind the eyes, in the coils of the brain, in the porous marrow of bone, in the busy traffic of the stomach, anywhere in any live body will do cancer for starters.

'Mr R., fifty-six, has colon cancer,' Stuart begins in a brisk monotone. 'He's in for symptom control. Also has neuropathic pain in the right leg. Radiation has shrunk the pelvic mass but made no difference to the pain.'

'He feels *he's* let the side down because *he* didn't get rid of the pain,' says Dr Peter Martin, his rich Irish voice filled with irony. 'He has a daughter who needed to take a holiday. He assured her he was feeling fine, so she went off to Perth and he sat at home with his leg up. His diagnosis? Terrible. A number of weeks. At best a couple of months.'

The table listens in silence.

'A cordotomy, maybe?' Michael asks.

'He's not there yet,' Stuart says. 'He came in three days ago and he's definitely more comfortable than then.' A cordotomy is a surgical procedure to sever the pain fibres from one side of the body. Although known for many years, the centre is re-evaluating cordotomies for certain types of difficult cancer pain. The procedure results in incontinence and can leave the patient paralysed but totally pain-free. 'We're still working on his medication,' Stuart continues. 'I'd like to see how he's doing in a couple of days. If he's still got a few weeks, he might prefer to keep walking for as long as he can.'

He puts the file aside and pulls out another. 'I think we could send Mrs B. home.' Mrs B., Wyona, is twenty-eight, with a husband, a five-year-old child, and a right frontal mass in her brain. 'She has a syringe driver and no pain. We can't do anything further for her here.'

'What's the situation at home?' Michael asks.

'Well, the husband hasn't been visiting much,' says Kelly, the head nurse. 'I think you spoke to him, Barbara?'

Barbara nods. 'He's having a very hard time coming to terms with what's happening. Their relationship has been good. He's just grieving deeply. It's all a nightmare for him. He's been staying with his in-laws who've been looking after the child. If Wyona goes home, it will be to her parents. The only difficulty could be Wyona's father. He refuses to believe she won't recover, which makes it very difficult for everyone else.'

Silence fills the room, allowing everyone to think about the case. Finally Barbara says, 'I'll be seeing the husband again tomorrow. I think moving her home would be a good idea. Her mother's there all the time, and if Wyona could be cared for at home, it would make it a lot easier for her.'

Wyona is marked for discharge and Stuart moves on to the next case. 'Mr C., fifty-two, metastatic melanoma. Unknown primary site. It's now behind both eyes. His voice is getting hoarse. He's comfortable with subcutaneous needles.'

'He's a very happy chap,' Jill says. 'Does he know how bad it is?'

'No, he thinks it's five past eleven,' a woman's voice says. I can't locate the speaker.

'Don't you think he'd want to know?' Jill asks. 'He might like to arrange things.'

'Maybe you could see where he's at,' Michael says to Peter, who nods in agreement.

Stuart shakes his head. 'The next two cases…Mrs D. is forty-three with colon and pelvic cancer and a long history of drug addiction. She has a twelve-year-old daughter, very mature, looks more like twenty. As you'll recall, we tried to get Mrs D. onto methadone, but no way.' Methadone is a synthetic opioid drug that is used extensively in drug-dependence rehabilitation programs. It is also sometimes used in pain management for a few patients who do not tolerate morphine very well. 'She said it suggested she was an addict!'

'It's difficult to know how much pain she's having,' Dr Kate Jackson says, 'or how much of her demand is just drug dependency. She's comfortable and actually could go home. But I'm pretty concerned about what she'll do with any drugs we give her.'

'Who'd look after her and the daughter?' Gabrielle, a nurse consultant, asks.

'She has a sister who wants to provide care, but she's an addict, too,' Barbara replies.

'Wasn't she supposed to have a cordotomy?' Gabrielle asks.

'She's developed a bowel obstruction,' Peter says. 'She's a nonstop smoker and wouldn't survive the anaesthetic.'

'The real difficulty is with the daughter,' Jill says. 'She told a relative she was staying here with her mother, and she told us she was staying with that relative.'

'Well, where has she been staying?' Michael asks, a tinge of urgency in his voice.

'We don't know,' Nurse Michelle explains. 'She's very good at making things up apparently. In this present set-up she has total freedom. Her relatives think she's sleeping here. We think she's with her relatives. But she could be on the street.'

Michael says flatly, 'We can't be responsible for a twelve-year-old. Is Mrs D. aware of what her daughter's doing?'

'We just found out ourselves,' Michelle replies. 'I doubt Mrs D. can control her daughter. Her son came yesterday with handcuffs on and a guard on each side. He'd been allowed out of prison for a couple of hours to see his dying mother. He's only nineteen. He cried all the way back down the driveway when he left. I went in to see Mrs D. because I thought she'd be upset too, but she wasn't. She gave me the impression motherhood isn't her strong point.'

'Sounds like it's time for Mrs D. to be discharged,' Michael says. 'Her pain is under control and she wants to leave. We can only do so much and we've done it.'

'I'll contact Dandenong palliative care,' Gabrielle says, 'and tell them what the situation is so they can keep close tabs on her drug intake. I'll also let them know about the daughter. Maybe they can arrange something.'

'Who's next?' Stuart asks, pulling out a file. 'Yes, Mrs E. This patient has galloping brain cancer and marrow cancer. She's here from Pakistan with her three children so they can attend university. Her husband works in South Africa but is coming here next week. I'm afraid he's in for a terrible shock. I doubt he knows how sick she is. She has no idea how bad it is herself. There's a language difficulty in treating her. She went home last night without telling anyone. Jennie phoned her at home when we found she'd gone. She came back a couple of hours ago.'

Stuart pauses, then continues. 'The main difficulty is religious. She won't take either liquid morphine or shots. She believes she shouldn't take any pain relief. She's Muslim, and apparently believes that if Allah has sent her suffering she must endure it. I've told her that there's no point in her being here if she won't let us help her. Anyway, we've now got her on a fentanyl patch. She agreed to that. I explained that it was a morphine derivative, although I'm not totally certain she understood.'

A deep sigh is heard, a wave of exhaled compassion that fills the room.

'What about her children?' Jill asks. 'Have they said anything about it?'

'I spoke to them,' Nurse Jennie replies. 'They said they respected their mother's wishes and would wait for their father to arrive. They only come every third or fourth day, probably because they can't cope with seeing their mother so miserable. She's very psychologically and socially distressed. A few members of the Pakistani community have visited her, but we've all got our fingers crossed waiting for the husband to get here.'

'I'd like to be told as soon as that happens,' Michael says. 'His views might be different. We don't want to do anything contrary to her religious beliefs.'

'I made sure she knew it was a fentanyl patch,' Stuart insists. 'She knows fentanyl is a painkiller. Maybe her prohibitions are simply against needles or oral medication.' He sighs in frustration. 'I just don't know.'

Case by case, I am given a close-up look into the complexities of palliative care management of end-of-life problems in a multicultural society. In the Dandenong district, as one example, 27 per cent of patients don't speak English, and the lack of competent medical interpreters is an ongoing difficulty. As Stuart finishes his list, I realise that the problem is not simply a matter of obtaining interpreters, but of finding interpreters who are competent in medical terms and deeply familiar with both cultures. Each culture has its own way of explaining and treating ill health, particularly dying, and social and cultural factors play a powerful role in both what is interpreted and the way in which it is interpreted. Cultural factors also play a part in a patient's response to suggested symptomatic or pain control.

That afternoon I have a long interview with Dr Michael Ashby. Since arriving at McCulloch House, I have been waiting for the chance to explore his personal and academic background to find out what led him into this world of suffering and pain control.

We begin our talk over a lunchtime sandwich at a small Italian delicatessen near the Clayton train station. Although Michael appreciates the finer aspects of life and is fully informed in the world of art, music, language and literature, his packed working hours allow no time for a long and leisurely lunch. I ask him about his life history, and for a while he recounts it with detached good humour, as if he were the observer rather than the subject, batting forth his responses with precision, ease and a few laughs—some directed at life, some at himself.

He was born in 1954 in Surrey, England, and raised in the small town of Horley, equidistant from London and Brighton. His younger brother, Nicholas, now a financial analyst living in Malaysia, was born three years later. In those days Horley was a small, sleepy village, but because of the railway station it grew rapidly and eventually Gatwick Airport was built nearby, changing the character of the area forever.

'My mother, Gwyneth, is Australian, brought up in Carnegie, which at that stage was at the edge of the known world of Melbourne,' Michael tells me. 'She and my father, who was English, were married in Ormond in 1952 and then they took off for England for a year. My mother's still there forty-five years later.'

When Michael was nine the family went to live in France. This move was to have a subtle but lasting effect on his life. The house the Ashbys took was in Flanders, on the Franco-Belgian border, where their friends and neighbours worked for the War Graves Commission. Because of the proximity of the Belgian and French war graveyards, Michael spent hours on his bike riding around them. The image of the orderly rows and rows of crosses was to remain with him.

'Two years later our lives changed enormously when my father was killed in a road accident in France. My mother, suddenly widowed and grieving in a foreign country, and with only a small command of the language, decided to return to our old house at Horley. I, and later Nicholas, was enrolled at Reigate, an old English country grammar school.'

Today Michael admits that the experience of living amid the solemn military graveyards along the Franco-Belgian border and, more intensely, the fact of his father's tragic and sudden death, had a lot to do with his later interest in the dying and the nature of death itself.

As a student, Michael was strong in the humanities and headed for a career in this area, probably in law. But when he was sixteen he got a part-time job in the district's Redhill General Hospital, where many of the medical staff had been trained at St Bartholomew's Hospital Medical College of the University of London, or Bart's, as it is better known. At Redhill Michael ended up cleaning and preparing the instrument trays for the operating theatre.

Always fascinated with doctors and medicine, he admits to having absolutely no idea that he would end up in the profession. However, when he was studying humanities for his A levels he found out about a pre-med year offered at Bart's. He was drawn to Bart's by a well-developed sense of history and a love of old places, an interest cultivated by grandparents who took both boys to endless National Trust sites in England. He won an entrance scholarship and in one arduous year completed all the science requirements.

Grants in England in those days were extremely generous and Michael received a virtually free education. He admits, with both a slight blush and a laugh, that he had no idea at the time of the enormity of the gift, despite his mother having raised both boys on a widow's pension. Perhaps the intensity of the work involved precluded all else.

Looking back, he sees himself as 'a very paternalistic and probably arrogant young doctor'. Some of the memories he has of encounters with patients and staff members 'horrify' him today, he says with a rueful grin, stopping to wonder aloud how much of his attitude arose from the fact that young doctors were poorly supported and the career structure was fiercely competitive.

'Anyway, I got through all that, graduated from Bart's, then trained in radiation oncology. I became a cancer specialist at the Royal Marsden Hospital in 1982. After that I went as clinical lecturer and honorary senior registrar to the Department of Clinical Oncology in Cambridge and was a tutor there for two years at the same time.'

It was at this time that his interest developed in medical education and, increasingly, in palliative care. His weekly teaching clinics at nearby Bedford General Hospital made him acutely aware of the number of patients in pain and how little could be done for them due to a shortage of time and resources.

'In 1987 I was lucky enough to get a fellowship for Peter MacCallum Cancer Institute here in Melbourne. I had long wanted to come and work in Australia, something almost certainly due to my mother's connection with this country. I spent a great deal of my time in the pain clinic, and it's significant at the time that it was very unpopular to work there. I remember the deputy medical general of the hospital being absolutely amazed that I wanted to go down there, because he had such difficulty attracting staff to go there. There I learnt the basics of pain control for patients with complex pain needs, and at that stage I really became hooked on this type of work.'

When the fellowship expired, Michael went to the Curie Institute in Paris and learned about implanting radioactive sources into tumours. However, before leaving Australia, he saw an advertisement for director of palliative-care services at the Royal Adelaide Hospital. He applied, and returned there as director of palliative-care services after his time in Paris. He also held the medical directorship of the Mary Potter Hospice at Calvary Hospital in North Adelaide. He had barely turned thirty-five.

'Those years, 1989 to 1995, were very formative. With fairly small resources I set up a palliative-care service with my colleague there, Dr Mary Brooksbank, and we built up a consult service in the Royal Adelaide Hospital, where we had a four-bed unit, as well as the sixteen-bed hospice unit at Mary Potter. So we were enormously busy with a continual demand for services.'

It was in this period that Michael became committed to palliative care, the development of its supportive services, and medical education. He became clinical senior lecturer in the Department of Medicine at Adelaide University, had an inaugural role at Adelaide Children's Hospital, and became involved in the home visiting of patients. So when the chair of palliative care was advertised at Monash University, which included the directorship of McCulloch House, Michael states he 'leapt at the opportunity'. In March 1995 Michael became professor of palliative care at Monash Medical Centre, though McCulloch House was not to open until February of the following year.

When I ask Michael how he perceives palliative care, he says, 'One of the documents that best sums up my views is the "Australasian Undergraduate Medical Palliative Care Curriculum", which I put together with my medical colleagues Mary Brooksbank, Paul Dunne and Rod McLeod. In that document we outline certain core values that underpin the proper care of people who are reaching the end of life.

'First, the best possible pain and symptom relief in clinical circumstances is both a patient's right and a doctor's duty. Second, dying is a natural part of living and death is an inevitable consequence of having life. No amount of medical progress can change this fact. As such, although we have a duty to try to preserve our patients' lives, this doesn't mean we are obliged to treat the dying as if they can be cured. Dealing with death and dying is an intrinsic part of medical practice, but we must guard against overmedicalisation of the process of dying.

'Third, grief, loss, and bereavement are fundamental parts of all of our lives, so an understanding of the patterns of human grief behaviour and the ability to understand and support grieving people is a core skill of being a doctor. Fourth, a person's dying days are just as valuable as his or her non-dying ones. Therefore, a person has a right to have his or her beliefs, needs and wishes recognised and respected at all stages of life, including when they're dying. Care should be based on viewing the patient's needs in the context of the whole person rather than as a series of medically defined parts. Appropriately, then, negotiated treatment abatement and symptom relief don't constitute causing death.'

While Michael finishes his lunch I think over what he's said. He is touching on the so-called 'double effect', a principle derided as expedient and hypocritical by proponents of euthanasia for reasons I have never understood. Our emotional, physical and intellectual lives are dominated by, and are subject to, intent. If I smack a child's hand as he puts it near a fire with the intent of teaching him that fire is dangerous, this action is entirely different to walking over to a child who is quietly and happily playing and smacking his hand. The action is identical but the intent is different. One action is motivated by love, the other by malice. Intent determines the nature of the act and its character and is an integral part of whatever results from it.

Michael gulps some mineral water and I take the opportunity to ask, 'How does all of this apply to McCulloch House?'

'Well, the main attraction of McCulloch House was a palliative-care unit located in an acute teaching hospital environment. And since the overall mission of a professor of palliative care is to bring about enduring change in the way decision-making and care at the end of life occurs, then we have to make sure this generation of medical students goes out into the workforce equipped with the attitudes, knowledge and skills required to do the job properly.

'That doesn't mean we think these students should, or can, be turned into palliative-care experts by such a short intervention in their course. In that time, though, they have one home visit with a community palliative-care nurse, one in-patient visit with a doctor or nurse and core case studies that illustrate specific points about pain management. They also have a debriefing group discussion about the patients they've met and the situations they've encountered. In those sessions I find that, unprompted, the students will raise nearly all of the pertinent issues concerning care of dying people either in the home or in an institutional setting.'

'And would pain control be one of those pertinent issues?' I ask.

Michael pushes his plate away and, taking off his glasses and wiping them with a cloth, says with quiet emphasis, 'Certainly. However, as I'm sure you're aware, there are a number of other symptoms, apart from pain, that cause people to despair and express a desire for assistance to die. If you look at palliative-care practice honestly, you'd have to say that some of our patients, despite the best care, have very difficult deaths. Just as there are no perfect births, there are no perfect deaths. Still, as palliative-care practitioners, we nearly always make a difference. It is extremely rare for us to be unable to do anything to assist patients in their symptom management or in their psychological, emotional or spiritual anguish. However, in medicine there are no perfect scores, and palliative care is just the same. We do have our limitations.'

'And your achievements?' I interject.

'Yes, one of those, I think, is the fact that we've made extensive inroads into dispelling the myth that opioid analgesia is addictive, and that if it is initiated too early there is nothing left for the end, a phenomenon known as tolerance.'

It is time, I think, to find out what Michael's views on euthanasia are, particularly as they relate to palliative care. 'Obviously the administering of opioids like morphine is an important element of pain control in terminal patients. Can pain management slip into actual euthanasia?'

Michael leans slightly across the table as he chooses his words carefully. 'A lot of doctors, and nurses, do feel responsible for causing death if they're involved in the use of opioids and sedatives in terminal care, or if they're involved in treatment-abatement decisions. In effect, they can still fear being seen as the cause of death. That's why we're very keen to promote good education about palliative care right across the health-care system, and certainly to ordinary graduating doctors.

'Still, I think it's very disappointing that the only means whereby we seem to be able to view death and dying in societal discourse and debate is through the optic of euthanasia. This is very limiting. All societies need to make sure that public policy allows doctors, nurses, and health-care teams to respond appropriately to people's suffering. In actual fact I have found politicians in Australia and Canada to be very sympathetic to the needs of dying people. I have never met anybody in public life who has had anything but helpful things to say about pain and symptom control and palliative care. Very few people dispute the fact that good care at the end of life is important. What we really need to do now is to concentrate on doing the care well, teaching, researching and acting as public advocates for palliative care.

'My personal view on euthanasia, though, is that while I have no ethical, legal, moral or religious arguments against legalising it, I would find it very difficult to be involved in it. I take this reluctance very seriously. I am not involved in measures that would have the intention of actively ending life. However, I'm very open with patients in discussing what we can't do with regard to voluntary active euthanasia or physician-assisted suicide. The vast majority of patients accept this. In fact, it's very unusual to have enduring anger or disappointment expressed to the treating staff in the palliative-care unit after these kinds of conversations.'

We both mull over Michael's last words as a train screeches into the station, making further conversation impossible. The intrusion of the everyday world prompts us to leave our hurried meal and return to McCulloch House along noisy Clayton Road. As we walk, I comment, 'From what you've told me about the education aspect of palliative care, you seem to be quite optimistic about the future.'

'There are wrinkles still to work out, of course,' he replies, 'but we now have a palliative care curriculum. We've integrated palliative care into the undergraduate program, and a rotation of three weeks in palliative care is a requirement of any doctor going into physical medicine. Nevertheless, that doesn't mean there isn't a great deal of work still to be done in changing attitudes towards death and dying. But it's all slowly coming together.'

When it does come together, it won't be a moment too soon. Browsing through the 'Australasian Undergraduate Medical Palliative Care Curriculum' that night, I note this chilling sentence: 'Demographic and epidemiological trends indicate that one in four Australians and New Zealanders now die of cancer, a proportion which will rise to one in three during the first decade of next century. Palliative care is therefore not a peripheral activity or a special interest group.'

Why do so many practitioners still know little about palliative care and display little interest in finding out about it? Most doctors are drowned in a flood of endless information: newsletters, pamphlets, Internet printouts, seminars and research papers. Like the rest of us, they only have twenty-four hours in each day; unlike many of us, they are called upon to make one decision after another, some that are critical.

Despite the prestigious position that society generally grants to doctors, they remain part of, and usually a product of, the society in which they work. The most common responses to death and dying in our society are fear and denial. Could the failure of doctors to show greater interest in the accelerating palliative-care movement simply reflect accepted societal attitudes combined with a chronic shortage of time?

I recall a conversation I had with Stuart Moir, the doctor doing his residency in physician training. 'The theme that underlines medical school is saving people,' Stuart told me. 'So we do a lot of interventions in cancer, and people with only one or two weeks to live often spend it in post-operative pain. We know they won't live, but the subconscious teaching that says you must always try to do something is very deep. It's hard to do what they do here—just make the patient comfortable and let him go. That's not most doctors' cup of tea.'


My time at McCulloch House is almost up. I can see how limited and inadequate, even naive, my initial question was: *Is euthanasia necessary or can accessible palliative care supplant the need for it?* I had thought that palliative care, perfected and accessible to all, might provide the answer. But it doesn't. It provides a magnificent answer for the majority of terminally ill people, but the majority of people are not the nub of the problem. The nub is really the 5 to 8 per cent of patients whose pain is beyond the control of today's palliative and pharmacological knowledge.

What is the question I should have asked? Something like: *Should a rigidly circumscribed law be drafted that permits patient-requested euthanasia in cases where all palliative care practices to control pain have been unable to do so?* Perhaps, although I remain dissatisfied with this question too. I am more convinced than when I started this book that if euthanasia is permitted someone will be killed who still wants to live, even though others might judge the victim's life not worth living or his or her suffering to be more than a human should endure. I am equally convinced that the research required to find the solution to extreme pain in all cases will never be done if euthanasia is permitted simply because it is the cheapest and easiest solution in a world where health budgets are tight, solutions are judged by practical results, and moral standards are determined, essentially, by expediency. This moral elasticity, which translates into expediency, is endemic in most societies today. It is as evident in the decisions made by heads of governments as in the lyrics of the punk-rock world.

Yet there is a hard truth at the heart of the euthanasia question: the reality of pain. I am thinking of real pain, not the fear and anger that is in the minds of those who, until they become terminally ill, live under the illusion that they 'own' their bodies and can determine all life-and-death issues for themselves. Such people, in order to prove they are masters of their own destinies, seek to end their lives through euthanasia.

I could see with Sue Rodriguez, and later with Graham Davey, how authentic their psychological suffering was, how valid and completely understandable their desire to maintain dignity and independence. Yet the desire to end one's life if physical pain is under control arises mainly from illusion—the illusion that *all* suffering can be avoided, the illusion that exercising one's will to do so is an inherent expression of one's humanity and dignity. The time I spent with Yvonne Linden, Harry Symonds, and the family of Tony Dimattina, among many others, showed me that life can't be lived entirely on our own terms. In fact, learning that such an insight is a reality is an essential part of our becoming fully human. So I conclude that to bring in legislation that would cater to a view of life that eviscerates life's deepest potential would be a form of social suicide.

Yet, whether I am right or wrong, this conclusion does absolutely nothing to help the 5 to 8 per cent who are terminally ill, who are in uncontrollable pain, and who request euthanasia. These sufferers, whom any one of us might be destined to join, are the valid heart of the euthanasia problem. Questions of legal rights, human rights, autonomy of choice and preservation of dignity become peripheral in the face of their suffering, and questions of morality assume a more profound complexity.

For the moment I decide to set this problem aside in an effort to determine why so many others, whose pain is controllable, are dying bad deaths. Ploughing through the Internet and various medical libraries, I find a wide agreement among experts that the world of the ill, particularly the aged and the terminally ill, is one characterised by unnecessary suffering. The two main elements that sustain this existence of misery are poor communication between doctor and patient, and under-treatment with morphine and other analgesics.

One of the most striking examples of the medical profession's failure to understand the nature and effect of severe pain is contained in a classic study conducted by Eland and Anderson of the University of Iowa in 1977. They found that more than half of the children four to eight years old who underwent major surgery, including limb amputation, excision of a cancerous neck mass, and heart repair, were given *no* medication for relief of their post-operative pain. The remainder received inadequate doses. The reason: not only did health-care workers fear addicting the children, *but they did not believe children felt pain as intensely as adults.* An eight-year-old has his leg amputated and he doesn't feel enough pain to merit any relief? Didn't any of these doctors or nurses have children? Or is it that once a child becomes their patient they are no longer seen as a child but only as a disease?

Dr Ronald Melzack refers to the above study in his *Scientific American* article, 'The Tragedy of Needless Pain'. He points out that the elderly also pay the penalty of ignorance:

> In a study of post-surgical pain, my colleagues and I found that surgical wards contain two basic populations: a young and middle-age group that recovers quickly and an older group whose pain remains severe and lingers for many days beyond the normal three- to four-day recovery period. Despite the persistent high level of pain in these older patients (presumably because of complications that arise after surgery), and despite a longer recovery period, they do not receive larger doses or a higher daily amount of medication. About 30 per cent of the patients on a surgical ward at any time fall into this older category.*

In a similar vein the *New York Times* of 30 June 1997 described a study first published two years earlier. It recorded that among 9000 acutely ill patients in teaching hospitals, half had spent their dying days in moderate or severe pain. This occurrence resulted from the fact that 'many doctors simply do not know how to prescribe properly the extraordinarily high doses of narcotics that some dying people need.'**

So pain is the problem. It is the energy-creating force behind the push for euthanasia. Why has the medical profession never systematically attempted to defeat the worldwide problem of acute and chronic pain? Recent medical literature suggests

* Ronald Melzack, 'The Tragedy of Needless Pain', *Scientific American*.
** Editorial, 'When Will Adequate Pain Treatment Be the Norm?', *Journal of American Medical Association*.

several factors. The treatment of pain was not as high a priority as the treatment of disease. Dependence and tolerance of analgesics does not imply addiction, but many doctors are unaware of this clear distinction. Organised religion is worried about two ethical issues—the impairment of a patient's cognitive functions prior to death so that one cannot spiritually 'prepare' for it, and the belief that pain medication may hasten death.

In our delicatessen talk, Dr Michael Ashby mentioned the false beliefs that surround opioid use and how, in McCulloch House, the practice is to give as much medication as needed to defeat pain, with no top limit. Most medical literature supports Dr Ashby's convictions and mode of palliative-care practice, although in some countries, including the United States, there are medical practitioners who still regard morphine as dangerous as the devil. One authority who does not is Dr A. G. Lipman of the Pain Management Centre of the University of Utah's university hospital. He contends that 'myths' surround the use of opium and until these are challenged and rejected there is little possibility of patients receiving appropriate analgesics in doses sufficient to relieve pain. His ten 'myths' include six that are highly relevant to palliative care.*

> Myth 1: *There is a maximum safe dose of morphine and other opioids.*
> Not so, says Lipman. Adjusting the amount of medication to the patient's response is the only way to determine, with consistency and reliability, the optimal amount for a specific patient.
>
> Myth 2: *Opioids cause addiction and therefore must be used with great restraint.*
> Lipman holds that this is not true. He maintains that while

* A. G. Lipman, 'Opioid Use in the Treatment of Pain: Refuting Ten Common Myths', *Pain Management*.

dependence among abusers and recreational users does occur, it is nonetheless rare when treating opioid-responsive pain patients.

Myth 3: *All those receiving opioids rapidly become tolerant and need their doses continually increased.*

Lipman says that, on the contrary, in many advanced cancer patients dose requirements decrease as frequently as they increase. An increase in dose is more often indicative of progressive disease rather than tolerance. Although tolerance occurs, it does so early in the opioid therapy and need not be a clinical problem.

Myth 4: *If morphine is used early in the disease, there will be nothing left to treat the pain later.*

Again Lipman's research indicates otherwise. Morphine, Lipman notes, has a straight-line, dose-response curve, which means that the dose and the response to it maintain a stable relationship so that morphine doses can be increased indefinitely and effectively in proportion to the intensity of pain.

Myth 5: *Patients who demand too many opioid doses are becoming tolerant or addicted.*

Lipman notes the great variations that exist in the amount of drugs different individuals require for pain relief. Although Lipman admits there might be an occasional patient who 'scams' the system to obtain opioids, this does not provide a reason for other patients to suffer unnecessary pain.

Myth 6: *Patients who complain of another pain once their initial pain has been successfully treated are probably drug abusers.*

This is not so, says Lipman. There are many other reasons for a new complaint of pain. He points out that one pain may mask another, and notes that over one-third of cancer patients have pain from four or more different causes or origins.

What is the situation in Australia, and how accessible are pain-relief services? Palliative-care services exist in most parts of Australia in some form. By and large, doctors in Australia can get advice and support in the control of severe pain at least by telephone if they are motivated to do so and if they know how to access experienced palliative-care practitioners. But the picture painted by Dr J. Norelle Lickiss, a palliative-care specialist at Sydney's Prince Alfred Hospital, isn't reassuring:

> We know on an anecdotal basis that cancer pain relief is not universally satisfactory in Australia. The list of barriers to widespread good quality cancer pain relief in Australia does not include availability of opioids, but rather the following: (a) failure to assess patients adequately, not only because of limited clinical knowledge and skills, but also because of language and cultural barriers; (b) continuing inappropriate use of analgesic drugs, or use of inappropriate drugs; and (c) failure to refer patients (in hospital clinic, nursing home or home) to palliative care or other relevant services in circumstances where pain relief is poor, either because the assessment has been inadequate or because there is still lack of realisation that cancer pain is, on the whole, treatable.*

A world of terrible and unnecessary pain lies behind this calm assessment. It is a world that is changing, but not fast enough to ensure a 'good as possible' death for all who read this book. We must determine to accept death as an ordinary part of life, something none of us will escape. We must determine to accept some suffering as an ordinary part of life. But we must also determine that extreme and prolonged pain has no place in a society that prides itself on its social and humanitarian standards.

* J. N. Lickiss, 'Australia: Status of Cancer Pain and Palliative Care', *Journal of Pain and Symptom Management*.

# The End and the Beginning

*We shall not cease from exploration*
*And the end of all our exploring*
*Will be to arrive where we started*
*And know the place for the first time.*
  —T. S. Eliot, 'Little Gidding'

I sit at my desk in the green-lamped, nineteenth-century splendour of the reading room in the State Library and try to read. Today is my last day at McCulloch House. I have loved every moment of this intense experience, have devoured every day and felt stretched an inch further every night. I realise how deeply all the acts of terrorism, war and racial hatred that have plagued the world during the past thirty years have affected me, weakening my idealism and discouraging my faith in people.

McCulloch House has helped restore that faith. I have taken the violence and hatred too much to heart, allowed the raucous voices too long a hearing, given their quarrelsome ways too much attention and time. They are just a part of the story of our times, not *the* story, despite their dominant role in the media. Creative energy and love are still powerful forces on this planet, too integral to all life to be limited or contained. Given an atmosphere that makes room for them, they can re-create the world around them. If I said that it is like glancing into paradise to witness the unconditional love that palliative caregivers strive for in their work, you might think it an exaggerated reaction, but I consider it an accurate description.

The processes of palliative care were only part of the equation when I accepted the writer-in-residency at McCulloch House. The problem haunting me since the physician-assisted suicide of the Canadian, Sue Rodriguez, is my need for a definitive, final, absolute answer on the question of euthanasia. Sue was not in physical pain when she killed herself. Is it because of this, because of the element of haste, even expediency, that I find her action morally repugnant? Or is it because I do not believe we own our own lives?

Yet I can't claim this assertion as an absolute belief without being a hypocrite. If a child close to me was terminally ill, in dreadful, uncontrollable pain and wanting death, I would ask that she or he be given a fatal dose. If an adult close to me was in a similar situation and was repulsed by, and terrified of, being put into a deep opioid sleep until death occurred—which is the accepted solution today for the approximately 5 per cent whose pain cannot be controlled—I suspect I would ask for euthanasia for him or her. As for myself, I like to think I could tough it out on the principle that I don't own my life, but I have experienced enough prolonged and extreme pain to suspect this is a fantasy.

At the same time I am convinced that if the ethic of euthanasia is accepted, people who may not want to die may have this decision taken from them by relatives or medical staff.

In an attempt to find an answer I had formulated the question: *Is euthanasia desirable or necessary, or could accessible palliative care supplant the need for it?* Much later, as I learned for myself that palliative care cannot as yet solve all problems of pain, I reformulated the question: *Should a rigidly circumscribed law be drafted that permits patient-requested euthanasia in cases where all palliative care practices to control pain have been unable to do so?*

I am tremendously surprised that I want to say yes, surprised because I believe we are created beings; we do not own our lives. Euthanasia is morally wrong, yet I have concluded that in some cases refusing to grant it can be a greater wrong, that euthanasia can be the right thing to do. If there is a hierarchy of values in the realm of the good, there is also a hierarchy of values in the realm of the bad.

There is nothing like spending time with the dying to get one's priorities and one's perceptions straight. My perception of life as a spiritual journey has been clarified and consolidated by all that I have seen at McCulloch House. There I witnessed first-hand what the writer-philosopher William James called 'the varieties of religious experiences', people struggling to deal with a cosmic consciousness through the simple actions and events of their daily lives.

There is a certain irony in my conclusion, because it is predominantly those who express their love and 'spirituality' in humanitarian activities, minus any God, who support euthanasia. I, on the contrary, believe that our lives are lock, stock and barrel a spiritual journey. It is a matter of individual experience and conscience how we achieve our potential, a matter that precludes the imposition of forced suffering on a dying person, one that demands at all times that we act with compassion, even if acting compassionately requires a decision that calls for the highest degree of trust.

I am content with my conclusion that euthanasia is morally wrong but is sometimes the right thing to do. Why then can I not endorse it? Why do I believe there should be no changes in the current laws to grant doctors or anyone else advance legal authority to terminate life? Euthanasia can seem to be, and actually can be, a compassionate and loving act. What is not obvious to me is that it necessarily follows that compassion should be the overruling consideration when an individual or a society decides how to act. And that is what this question comes down to—the insoluble dilemma of the tension between the individual and the state, between compassion as a private individual act and compassion as a foundation for social policy. What is good for one individual is not necessarily good for society.

When public policy is formulated, it is meant to act as a cohesive, stabilising force in the pattern of values that are deeply woven into our culture—in this case, that human life, because of the nature of mankind, needs to be protected in all circumstances. I see now that this is where Sue Rodriguez and I split. This is the source of my discomfort with her suicide.

Sue felt that compassion provided a justification sufficient for legalising euthanasia in her case. I understood Sue's needs and, because I admired and respected her as an individual, I was deeply torn. But Sue lost me when she showed no understanding of, or interest in, the way her highly publicised legal struggle might impact on others. She appeared to feel no significant relationship with her community or with society at large. The highest value in her life was her autonomy, the freedom to follow her individual subjective preferences. She appeared to assume that all values were merely personal, the product of each person exercising his or her autonomous will. There were no rational, objective judgments. There were only 'values' that arose out of perceived need, emotion, psychological complexes, attitudes, all produced by one's upbringing or life situation.

But Sue was only partly right. Some people use their

freedom to create happy satisfactory lives for themselves and others don't. Some people act wisely, morally, justly, charitably towards others and some don't. Communities and societies are held together, no matter how imperfectly, by commonly accepted, transcendent ideals such as justice, charity and objective truth. When these ideals are set aside to make room for the unlimited exercise of personal autonomy—of which euthanasia would be one expression—will the lives of the handicapped be secure, will the aged be protected, will the wishes of the terminally ill who do not want euthanasia carry as much weight as the individual wishes of the powerful and healthy? What of the lonely, the depressed, the mentally ill? Who will speak for them then? If euthanasia were legalised, can every person in our society be always counted on to act morally if faced with the care and responsibility of a terminally ill relative or friend, a responsibility that could endure for years? The answers to these questions may be found in the Dutch experience.

The situation in the Netherlands is often cited as a reflection of that country's enlightened and compassionate society. However, testimony given by the Dutch Physicians League before the British House of Lords Committee on Medical Ethics does not support this image: 'What public support there was for euthanasia [came from] clever campaigning by the media and by the Dutch Voluntary Euthanasia Society. Many who supported euthanasia did so after witnessing the painful dying of relatives or friends, *but this could be avoided by concentration on improved treatment.*'*

While the practice of euthanasia has gained the Netherlands a worldwide reputation for its liberal and humanistic stance,

* Lords Committee, 'Report of the Select Committee on Medical Ethics' [author emphasis added].

what is not known is that the Netherlands has almost no palliative care and that among its European peers it is considered one of the great laggards in addressing end-of-life suffering—other than terminating it. 'The evidence for this,' Dr Paul Henteleff told a Canadian Senate special committee, is that 'the use of pain-relieving drugs is relatively so small in the Netherlands, compared with countries where palliative care is good, that [terminally ill patients] could not possibly be getting even basic symptom relief as a basis for which care can be given.'*

This low use of pain-relieving drugs suggests that once the ethic of euthanasia is accepted, the ethic of care and the concept of helping the terminally ill live fully until death become redundant. To both the patient in pain, and the doctor who lacks pharmacological knowledge and palliative care skills, euthanasia must look like the only and final solution. And, with the passage of time, the practice of euthanasia will inevitably assume an aspect of normality.

I have struggled with my confusion. Do I lack faith? Have I no respect for the great traditional religions of the world that for 2000 years have argued against euthanasia? Have I no decent, godly 'fear of the Lord'? I am caught in the position of maintaining that we are not the owners of our lives while in a few cases might be willing to act as if we are.

Yet it is clear that much of the cruelty and human madness on this planet springs from ideas that our own intellects have constructed. We seize on concepts and notions, arising in our limited minds, and attribute to them the power of absolute truths. Then we feel compelled, for whatever narcissistic reason,

* Paul Henteleff, 'Proceedings of the Senate Special Committee on Euthanasia and Assisted Suicide'.

to act them out, impose them on others. The Crusades, the Inquisition, the Third Reich, Pol Pot's Cambodia, Indonesia's depredations in East Timor, China's brutality in Tiananmen Square, civil war in Rwanda, the bloodbaths of 'religious', political and ethnic cleansing in Europe, South America and Africa illustrate this truth.

These inhuman, ungodly bloodbaths have one thing in common: the total absence of compassion. If compassion was present, there could not have been any autos-da-fé, no one would have built concentration camps, no Holocaust would have occurred, no Chinese troops would have driven tanks over unarmed Chinese students, no Hutus or Tutsis would have clubbed one another's children to death. If we choose to ignore compassion, refuse to acknowledge that it is part of our humanity *for a reason,* we do so at our own peril. When we mistake compassion for weakness and expediency, when we shove it aside and discount it, give it no place or respect, the vacuum left in our heads and hearts fills up with a righteousness that, protected under the guise of religion, can constitute a devilish inhumanity.

Psychologically I understand those who initiate these horrors, since I share, to some extent, one of their characteristics. This is a spontaneous need to feel right, to be certain that my stance is the correct one. In the process of seeking an answer to the question of euthanasia, that characteristic has been very much in evidence. I have sought a clear-cut belief that will hold up in every case, leave me without the pain of doubt, even infuse me with a sense of superiority. I wanted the comfort, the security of an absolute value, an open-and-shut mind-set that would leave me in peace forever.

Then I asked myself: what must be the ideas and feelings that dominate a person who, when faced with someone in extreme agony and asking for death, closes their mind and heart? Are they disguising their fear of doing wrong under the guise of faith? Is it a form of self-concern: 'You can suffer till hell freezes over, but I am not risking losing my soul for you?' Is it a healthy fear of being terribly wrong, or does religion provide an excuse to do nothing? Is a refusal to help not only a lack of courage, an unwillingness to take any sort of risk, but even a lack of real faith, a lack of that most fundamental of all dispositions in a spiritual life—an abiding sense of trust?

I realise I have been seeking something that I will never find, something that doesn't exist on this earth, something we are not meant to have. Our love of answers, neat equations, wrapped-up conclusions, all arising from ego, lead us to think that order is preferable to chaos. We are meant to struggle with this question, to wonder, worry, even torment ourselves with it. As some bioethicists have suggested, perhaps the challenge will be to withhold social and legal approval for euthanasia so that life isn't cheapened, while at the same time allowing enough flexibility in law to recognise euthanasia as an ethically tolerable act in strictly circumscribed situations.

This is the 'slippery slope' that comes with any acceptance of euthanasia. But I believe it is one we must accept and legally, ethically, master. We live in a universe of such space and time, of galaxy after galaxy, that the best of our minds cannot conceive of it. We are meant to do what we think is the best at the moment that we do it, and we are meant to suffer and struggle with the rights and wrongs of that action. In this process of struggle we remain aware of our limits, we become more fully human, we build a life on trust and a life of true faith.

A voice cuts my thoughts short: 'The library is now closing. Will all visitors please make their way to the Swanston Street exit.'

People push through the front doors of the library into a night where the gusty rain stabs like Antarctic ice. I hurry along Swanston Street to the Victorian grandeur of Flinders Street Station. Young people huddle in doorways, smoking, talking, hanging out, going nowhere. Neon lights in tired shop windows wash their faces in sickly hues of red and blue. Dead leaves and wrappings clog the gutters and build up like sodden cardboard against the drainage grills. Cars creep along, drivers squinting through thumping windscreen wipers, dazzled by the barrage of lights in the oily treacherous streets. People push by, shoulders hunched like boxers entering the ring.

Somewhere a siren wails. Some human being in trouble, some human being to the rescue. An image of McCulloch House comes to mind, the halls now quiet, the doors closed on rooms where families and nurses are accompanying a patient as far, as deep, as death allows the living. I realise that all over Australia, all over the world wherever palliative-care centres and services exist, there are similar scenes of love and loss, courage and comfort, of the best of modern medicine embracing with ease the mystery of death, offering mind and heart to make life good, to make it count, until the end.

Approaching Flinders Street I check out one of the clocks on the old yellow facade. Looking at my watch I realise that, if I run, if I can rouse the ticket clerk barricaded and invisible behind his wall, I might just make it.

# Bibliography

Abviven, Maurice, 'The Crisis of Dying', *European Journal of Palliative Care*, vol. 2, no. 1, 1996.

Addington-Hall, J. M. & Seale, C. 'Dying at the Best Time', *Social Science Medicine*, vol. 40, 1995, pp. 589–95.

Arras, John D. & Neveloff-Dubler, Nancy, 'Ethical and Social Implications' in *Bringing the Hospital Home: Ethical and Social Implications of High-Tech Home Care*, Arras, John D., (ed.), Johns Hopkins University Press, Baltimore, 1995, p. 18.

Ashby, Michael, 'Hard Cases, Causation, and Care of the Dying', *Journal of Law and Medicine*, vol. 3, no. 2, 1995, p. 157.

Birnie, Lisa Hobbs & Rodriguez, Sue, *Uncommon Will: The Death and Life of Sue Rodriguez*, Macmillan, Toronto, 1994.

Brown, Margaret, 'Medical Power of Attorney: A Benefit or Burden for the Well Elderly?', Masters Thesis, Flinders University of South Australia, 1995.

Chan, Arlene & Woodruff, Roger, 'Communication with Patients with Advanced Cancer Pain', *Journal of Palliative Care*, vol. 13, no. 3, 1997, pp. 29–33.

Fitzgibbon, D., Rapp, S. & Sullivan, M., 'Pain and the Choice to Hasten Death in Patients with Painful Metastatic Cancer', *Journal of Palliative Care*, vol. 13, no. 3, 1997, pp. 18–28.

Foley, R. M., et al, 'Character of Terminal Illness in the Advanced Cancer Patient: Pain and Other Symptoms During the Last Four Weeks of Life', *Journal of Pain and Symptom Management*, vol. 5, no. 2, 1990.

Frankl, Viktor, *Man's Search for Meaning: An Introduction to Logotherapy*, Pocket Books, New York, 1984, p. 98.

Hanks, G. W., 'Cancer Pain and the Importance of Its Control', *Anticancer Drugs 6*, April 1995, pp. 14–17.

Henteleff, Paul, 'Proceedings of the Senate Special Committee on Euthanasia and Assisted Suicide', Department of Supply and Services, Ottawa, 11 May 1994, p. 5.

'When Will Adequate Pain Treatment Be the Norm?', *Journal of American Medical Association*, vol. 274, no. 23, December 1995, pp. 1870–74, 1881.

Krause, Frances, 'Confronting the Reality of Terminal Illness', *European Journal of Palliative Care*, vol. 3, no. 4, 1997.

Lickiss, J. N., 'Australia: Status of Cancer Pain and Palliative Care', *Journal of Pain and Symptom Management*, vol. 12, no. 2, August 1996 pp. 99–101.

Lipman, A. G., 'Opioid Use in the Treatment of Pain: Refuting Ten Common Myths', *Pain Management*, vol. 4, no. 4, 1991, pp. 13–17.

Lords Committee, 'Report of the Select Committee on Medical Ethics', HMSO, London, 1994.

McIlhagga, Kate, in *Celebrating Women*, Ward, Wild and Morley (eds.), Morehouse Publishing, Harrisburg, 1995.

Melzack, Ronald, 'The Tragedy of Needless Pain', *Scientific American*, February 1990, pp. 27–33.

Monbourquette, Jean, 'Symbolic Death as Grief Therapy', *European Journal of Palliative Care*, vol. 3, no. 1, 1997.

Noddings, Nel, 'Moral Obligations or Moral Support' in *Bringing the Hospital Home: Ethical and Social Implications of High-Tech Home Care*, Arras, John D. (ed.), Johns Hopkins University Press, Baltimore, 1995, pp. 155–56.

Pullman, Darryl, 'Dying with Dignity and the Death of Dignity', *Health Law Journal*, University of Alberta, Canada, vol. 4, 1996, pp 197–219.

Sankar, Andrea, *Dying at Home: A Family Guide for Caregiving*, Bantam, New York, 1995.

Singer, Peter, *Rethinking Life and Death*, Text Publishing, Melbourne, 1996.

Wall, Patrick D., & Jones, Mervyn, *Defeating Pain: The War against a Silent Epidemic*, Plenum, New York, 1991, pp. 148–49.

Williams, Glanville, *The Sanctity of Life and the Criminal Law*, Knopf, New York, 1957.

THE FOLLOWING WEB SITES were used in preparing and writing this book. Each site is an excellent source for any reader who wants further information relating to pain management, opioids and palliative care.

American Academy of Hospice and Palliative Medicine: http://www.aahpm.org

American Society for Advancement of Palliative Care: http://www.asap-care.com

Euthanasia World Directory: http://www.efn.org/~ergo

International Association for the Study of Pain: http://www.weber.u.washington.edu/~crc/IASP.html

Palliative Care Council of South Australia: http://www.palcare.asn.au

Project on Death in America: http://www.soros.org/death.html

World Wide Congress on Pain Management: http://www.pain.com